INDOOR GRILLING
For Stovetop and Tabletop
Bob and Coleen Simmons

BRISTOL PUBLISHING ENTERPRISES, INC.
San Leandro, California

A Nitty Gritty® Cookbook

Printed in the United States of America.

ISBN 1-55867-096-3

Cover design: Frank Paredes
Cover photography: John Benson
Food stylist: Suzanne Carreiro
Illustrator: Kay Hogg

CONTENTS

INDOOR GRILLING

Man probably started to grill food soon after he learned to use fire for heat and light, and he has been grilling ever since. Cookouts and barbecues are a favorite way to party with family or friends, and it just isn't summer without firing up the grill. When the weather turns cooler and it starts to rain or snow, it is easy to move indoors with either electric and stovetop grills. The indoor grill really comes into its own when there is extreme fire danger, or if there isn't sufficient time to preheat the outdoor grill, or if one only wants to cook one or two portions of food. It is a quick, easy and convenient appliance for preparing a delicious, healthful meal.

There are several reasons to grill food indoors. All the fat can be removed from meats that are grilled indoors. Indoor grills need only a very short time to heat before the food to be grilled is added, and no charcoal starter or charcoal is needed. Cleanup of most indoor grills is very easy because there is little burned-on mess. Some of the grills have a nonstick coating of Teflon™ or Silverstone™, and several manufacturers suggest putting the racks and removable reflective pieces in the dishwasher.

We tested the recipes in this book on a variety of indoor grills. The open rack type proved to be the most versatile, especially when a screen or smaller mesh rack was used when grilling little vegetable and fish pieces that could fall through the larger rack spaces. The hinged grill, or clamshell, produced attractively browned foods, particularly when the items to be grilled were of an even thickness.

TYPES OF GRILLS

The most common and also the most versatile grills are the open electric countertop models. These have an electric coil one to two inches below a rack that holds the food being grilled. The higher the wattage coil, the better. There should be a reflective surface below the coil to radiate heat generated by the bottom of the coil back toward the food being grilled and also a place for juices that drip from the cooking food to flow so that they don't burn and smoke while the food cooks. You can further reduce the effect of any smoke by placing the grill under the vent hood on your stove. We put a cookie sheet on the burners to make a level, stable surface, and put the grill on that. Some of the more expensive grills have a heat control that allows the heat to be reduced for foods that require longer cooking. Some models have racks that can be raised or lowered, which is a desirable feature. Most electric grills have a very short electrical cord which demands the grill be placed close to an electric outlet.

The open countertop grill does a good job on irregularly shaped foods, such as kabobs, ribs, Cornish game hens, lobster tails, etc. The ultimate electric countertop grill is the Jenn-Air built-in. It has higher heat and a larger grilling surface than tabletop grills, with an efficient ventilation system to carry off any smoke or fumes. Countertop grills are almost smoke-free. The juices and fat that do drip from cooking food largely miss the glowing coil, and those juices that do hit the glowing coil vaporize almost immediately.

There are several stovetop grills that fit over a gas or electric burner. There are inexpensive cast iron models, often used for the Korean Bul Kogi, and newer nonstick models with a reservoir that can be filled with liquid to catch drippings before they can burn. These models are quite effective for flat foods such as strips of beef, flattened chicken breasts, thin fish fillets, sandwiches and sliced vegetables. The cast iron models, once hot, hold the heat longer, but are smaller in diameter.

Hinged electric grills, also called clamshells, do an excellent job on sandwiches, burgers, steaks and vegetables that are of uniform thickness. These grills cook quickly and evenly in about half the time of the open grill because heat is applied to both sides of the food at the same time. They either have channels to allow juices to run out, or a reservoir to catch them.

Some suggest adding a flavoring liquid to the reservoir, but we found this to have only a minimal effect on the taste of the food. Hinged grills tend to smoke more than the open or stovetop grills, and should be used under a stove hood or with good ventilation.

An indoor grill can be a great convenience and a handy appliance. It produces poultry, fish, meats and vegetables with an appetizing appearance with a minimum of time and effort. If your cooking surface is limited, an indoor grill can be very useful for cooking one or two items while the rest of the meal is prepared on the stove. The indoor grill is an excellent item of equipment for a vacation house or an apartment dweller.

TOOLS AND EQUIPMENT

There are several pieces of equipment that can make indoor grilling easier. Food cooks more quickly and evenly on an indoor grill when it is cut into small, regular sized pieces. The best way to control these small pieces is to put them on skewers. Wooden skewers are inexpensive, and make an attractive presentation on the platter or plate. There is a variety of metal skewers, some basic and functional, some decorated and very attractive. Metal skewers have the advantage of conducting heat into the center of the food, thereby allowing it to cook a little faster. There are very clever double skewers which keep the individual pieces from turning on the skewers. These usually have an insulated handle and a sliding pusher to assist in removing the cooked food. If you do a lot of grilling they are well worth seeking out.

One of the handiest tools to have is a pair of tongs. We like the professional type with leaf-shaped ends, 12 or 15 inches long. They allow the turning of various shaped items with ease.

There is a variety of mesh screens and grids that can be placed on the grill to allow smaller, more fragile foods to be grilled. The fine stainless steel screen works well, but can be difficult to clean. The enameled steel plate or "griffo" rack is perforated with small holes. It works quite well and is easier to clean.

All types of grills are much easier to clean if they are sprayed well with a nonstick cooking spray before using. This includes the inside of the grill where the drips fall from the cooking food, as well as the rack that holds the food. Try not to spray the heating coil. If you do, it will smoke for a minute as it heats.

MARINADES

A flavorful marinade tenderizes the low fat meat, fish and poultry that cook best on an indoor grill. Most marinades contain acid, usually vinegar, citrus juice or yogurt. The acid helps to tenderize, and in some cases partially "cook" the food. Red meats need more powerful marinades, and can be marinated for longer periods, even overnight. Chicken and fish only need to be marinated a few minutes, perhaps 4 hours maximum for chicken, and 30 minutes for fish. Red meat can be allowed to marinate at room temperature for up to 2 hours immediately prior to cooking. Chicken and fish should be marinated in the refrigerator, and only brought out about half an hour before grilling.

The best way to assure even marination is to place the food in a heavy self-sealing bag, pour in the marinade, exclude as much air as possible, and then zip the bag closed. This way most of the food will be in contact with the marinade. Just turning the package over will expose the rest of the food to the liquid.

Some grilled foods stand on their own, but many are greatly improved when served with a sauce. We have included sauces, salsas and other accompaniments for many of the recipes. Be creative.

SAFETY CONSIDERATIONS

Be sure to follow the manufacturer's instructions for your grill. Place the grill on a flat, stable surface. Don't put the grill where it can be pushed into a sink or easily knocked off the counter. Be sure not to let the cord hang over the counter edge where it can be brushed by an apron or pulled by a curious child.

Avoid the temptation to speed up cooking by covering an electric grill. The heat buildup may damage the grill, or even start a fire. Most manufacturer's instructions specifically say that the grill should not be covered.

Unplug the grill when not in use. Do not leave a heated grill unattended.

HINTS AND GENERALITIES

1.   To get great food from the grill you need to start with the freshest, highest

quality ingredients.

2. Always spray your grill with nonstick spray, and allow it to preheat for about 10 minutes or length of time specified by the manufacturer before putting the food on to cook.

3. Brush food lightly with olive oil or melted butter before placing on the grill if it hasn't been marinated.

4. Have a good "instant read" meat thermometer to check for doneness. Learn to test for doneness by poking the food with a finger. As meat and fish cook they tend to firm up; with practice you can learn to tell when food is cooked to the proper level. Thin slices of meat or ground meat will start to show droplets of moisture about the time they are half cooked, which indicates they are ready to be turned. Meat usually is cooked for slightly less time on the second side; a general guideline is about 60% of the time on the first side, 40% on the second.

5. Presoak wooden skewers 20 to 30 minutes before using to avoid burning the ends during the grilling process.

6. If you plan to serve both meat and vegetables on skewers, put the meat on one skewer and the vegetables on another, because of different cooking times. Thin squares of onion or peppers generally will cook about the same time as meat, and make an attractive looking presentation when alternated with the meat. Chunks of carrots or potatoes, unless partially precooked, may not cook as fast as the meat.

THE GRILLING PANTRY

Here are some items we like to keep on hand for quick and easy grilling.

OILS

A definite assist to quick and easy cleanup is nonstick cooking spray. There are several different kinds available on the shelf, including an olive oil spray. We try to remember to spray the cooking grill pan and the rack before every grilling event.

Olive oils are healthful and flavorful and you should consider keeping two different ones in the pantry: a light all-purpose oil for marinating delicate seafood dishes, and a fruity full-flavored oil for vegetables, poultry and salad dressings. We like the heavier full-flavored oil paired with herbs to give grilled foods a little extra complexity. Indoor grilling marinades have to make up for some of the smoky charcoal flavors produced by briquets and the hot barbecue flames. Full-flavored olive oils and fresh herbs are definite flavor enhancers. Buy only the amount of oil that you can use in a few weeks and keep olive oils tightly capped in a cool dark spot in your pantry.

VINEGARS

Vinegar keeps indefinitely so you can keep several in the pantry. Different vinegars have such distinctive characters that they can contribute significantly to the overall appeal of a dish. Apple cider, rice wine, red wine, tarragon wine and balsamic vinegar are great contributors to flavorful marinades.

MUSTARDS

Mustard can add a subtle nuance or be a major ingredient in marinades. Keep a Dijon, a stoneground, and some hot sweet mustard on hand. A distinctively flavored mustard is one of the quickest flavor enhancers for grilling. Savory large shrimp or chicken breasts are delicious when grilled with nothing more than a generous coating of flavorful mustard.

CHEESES

Shards of good Parmesan cheese are a terrific accent for grilled vegetables or a salad topping. Fresh goat cheese is wonderful in grilled eggplant sandwiches, and in a grilled tomato. You will want some full-flavored cheeses such as Gruyère and smoked Gouda for eggplant sandwiches and quesadillas.

HOT SAUCES AND RED PEPPER FLAKES

A dash or two of Tabasco, Crystal hot sauce, or your favorite green chile sauce brightens most sauces, marinades and dips. If you like spicy food, use a little more. Dried red pepper flakes are used in the same way — just a sprinkle to zip up the flavors.

OLIVES

Olives from the Mediterranean regions, either oil cured or brine cured, add a new dimension when chopped or served with various salads and vegetable dishes. Kalamata olives from Greece are a special favorite and are available at most Italian delicatessens as well as canned. Tiny black Niçoise olives are a perfect garnish for many salads and vegetable dishes.

SUN-DRIED TOMATOES

We prefer to use oil cured sun-dried tomatoes in the interest of time and flavor. These tomatoes keep indefinitely in the refrigerator and can be removed, thinly sliced and added to many dishes to provide a little flavor wallop. If you buy the bulk dried tomatoes, remember to rehydrate them in a little water or wine before using. Oil cured sun-dried tomatoes are great on kabobs to separate pieces of grilled meat, chicken or mushrooms.

WINE

Some delicious grilling marinades have some dry white wine as a base, particularly for fish or chicken. Vermouth or dry sherry are also good flavoring ingredients.

PROSCIUTTO

If you are using prosciutto as a wrapper, have it cut as thinly as possible. If imported Italian prosciutto is available, it is well worth the price. Very thinly sliced pastrami or baked ham make acceptable substitutes for prosciutto.

GRILLED APPETIZERS

Party time calls for some delicious morsels to get things rolling. Indoor grilling comes into its own for cooking small skewers of seafood, sausages, vegetable or meat roll-ups, and other goodies. Most appetizers take only a short grilling time, so with a little advance preparation it is easy to serve a tempting array of tidbits for a small group. Consider sharing the work and let your friends help assemble and participate in the grilling. Some of the most delicious appetizers are the simplest. So let's have a party!

Be sure to check the grilling tips on page 5.

PEARS WRAPPED IN PROSCIUTTO

Juicy ripe chunks of pear wrapped in thin slices of prosciutto and just warmed on the grill make a marvelous appetizer. The thinner the prosciutto, the better. Double or triple this recipe to meet the demand.

1 large ripe pear, Comice or Bartlett	coarsely ground black pepper
lime juice	5-6 thin slices of prosciutto

Peel and core pear and cut into quarters. Cut each quarter into 2 or 3 pieces. Sprinkle with lime juice and grind some black pepper over pieces. Divide each prosciutto slice approximately in half, lengthwise, and wrap around each piece of pear. Grill pieces on a preheated grill for 1 to 2 minutes per side, turning once, to lightly color prosciutto and warm pears. Serve immediately.

FIGS WRAPPED IN PROSCIUTTO

Fresh figs make a great appetizer also. When fresh figs are in season, buy the biggest, ripest ones you can find. Cut off stem and a small slice from the bottom; then cut into halves or quarters, depending on size of the fruit. Follow the directions for the **Pears Wrapped in Prosciutto**.

TERIYAKI BEEF AND VEGETABLE ROLLS

This is a great party appetizer!

1 lb. thin raw beef slices, about 2 oz. each
½ cup commercially prepared teriyaki sauce
1 tsp. grated fresh ginger
1 tsp. brown sugar

16 strips red or green bell pepper, ¼-inch wide by 4 inches long
16 strips carrots or green beans, ¼-inch wide by 4 inches long, blanched until crisp-tender, or strips of snow peas, thin asparagus, or thin green onion strips

Cut beef slices in half to make rectangles about 3 by 4 inches. Combine teriyaki sauce, ginger and sugar; marinate beef slices for 5 to 10 minutes. Remove meat from marinade and place 1 strip of pepper and 1 strip of carrot, green bean, or other vegetable, to make an attractive color combination, in the center of meat. Roll up into a tight bundle and secure with a toothpick placed parallel to meat seam. When the grill is hot, grill for 3 to 4 minutes each side, turning once. Remove from grill to a cutting board and allow to cool slightly. Trim ends and cut each roll into 3 to 4 pieces on the diagonal so colors of vegetables show. Serve with *Thai-Style Dipping Sauce*, page 23.

ASPARAGUS AND HAM ROLL-UPS

Makes: 8-16 pieces

Ham stuffed with bright green asparagus and mustard cheese sauce makes a deliciously different appetizer. Expand the recipe to meet the demand. If you have hearty eaters, serve whole rolls instead of cutting them.

8 thin slices cooked ham
Dijon mustard
1-2 green onions, white part only, finely minced
8 thin slices fontina or Swiss cheese
8 medium spears crisp cooked fresh asparagus

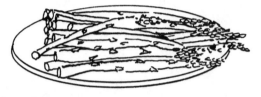

Spread ham slices lightly with Dijon mustard. Sprinkle a little green onion in center of ham. Top with cheese and asparagus. Asparagus should be longer than ham slice so top and bottom of asparagus show. Roll into a fairly tight roll and place a toothpick through center to hold the roll closed. Grill for 1 to 2 minutes each side on a preheated grill. The rolls should be warm and the cheese slightly melted. Cut each roll in half to serve. Serve warm.

QUESADILLAS

Flour tortillas are great grilled alone. Brush one side with a little melted butter or olive oil and toast on the grill. Here are some suggestions for some delicious but not too authentic quesadilla fillings.

For each quesadilla

Brush 2 flour tortillas with melted butter or oil, optional
Spread 1 tortilla with:

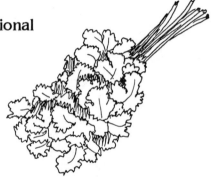

3-4 tbs. shredded Monterey Jack or cheddar cheese
1 tbs. grated Parmesan cheese
1-2 tbs. of your favorite fresh or bottled salsa
several fresh cilantro leaves

Top with remaining tortilla and place on preheated grill buttered or oiled side down. Grill for 2 to 3 minutes until just lightly browned, then turn quesadilla over and grill other side until cheese melts. Cut into quarters or eighths and serve while hot.

PESTO GOAT CHEESE QUESADILLAS

Servings: 1

This is a winning flavor combination.

For each quesadilla

Brush 2 flour tortillas with melted butter or oil, optional
Spread 1 tortilla with:

3-4 tbs. soft fresh goat cheese
2-3 tsp. prepared pesto
1 tbs. toasted pine nuts
1 tbs. grated Parmesan cheese

Top with remaining tortilla and grill as described on page 15.

DOUBLE TOMATO AND CHEESE QUESADILLAS

Make these in the summer with ripe tomatoes and fragrant sweet basil.

For each quesadilla

Brush 2 flour tortillas with melted butter or oil, optional

2-3 tbs. grated mozzarella cheese
1 tbs. grated Parmesan cheese
1-2 tsp. finely chopped green onion
1-2 small sun-dried tomatoes
  (oil packed or rehydrated), minced

1-2 tbs. chopped fresh salad tomatoes,
  seeded
4-5 small fresh sweet basil leaves, cut
  into ribbons
salt and freshly ground pepper

Sprinkle ingredients over 1 tortilla, top with other tortilla and grill as described on page 15.

HAM AND CHEESE QUESADILLAS

This makes a delicious, quick appetizer.

For each quesadilla

Brush 2 flour tortillas with melted butter or oil, optional

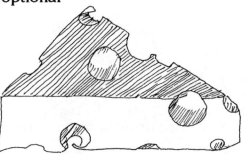

1 tbs. Dijon mustard
¼ cup grated Swiss or fontina cheese
1 tbs. grated Parmesan cheese
¼ tsp. dried tarragon or 1 tsp. chopped fresh
1 thin slice cooked ham, cut into ½-inch pieces

Spread 1 tortilla with mustard; then sprinkle on remaining ingredients. Top with other tortilla and grill as described on page 15.

CHINESE-STYLE CHICKEN WINGS

Pieces: 20

Savory chicken wings make great appetizers or picnic fare, and they freeze well. Marinate in a plastic bag for easy turning and cleanup.

10 chicken wings
2 tbs. soy sauce
1 tbs. vegetable oil
1 tbs. hoisin sauce
2 tsp. rice wine vinegar
1 clove garlic, finely minced
½ tsp. grated fresh ginger

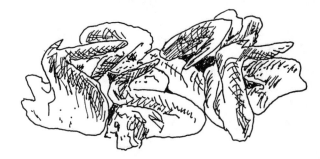

Prepare chicken wings by cutting off wing tips. Save them for chicken stock or another use. Separate wing into 2 pieces by cutting at joint. Cut off surplus skin at edge of pieces. Combine remaining ingredients, pour over wings and marinate in the refrigerator for 3 to 4 hours or overnight. Remove from refrigerator about 30 minutes before grilling. When ready to grill, drain and discard marinade. Grill for about 30 minutes on a preheated grill, turning 3 to 4 times, until golden brown and thoroughly cooked.

JERK SEASONED CHICKEN WINGS

These are spicy and delicious. Handle the jalapeño pepper very carefully, taking care when removing the stem and seeds. Wash your hands well after handling any hot pepper. Chicken wings are definitely finger food so serve with lots of napkins.

10 chicken wings
½ cup minced onion
1 jalapeño pepper, seeded, minced
2 tsp. soy sauce
1 tbs. vegetable oil
1 tbs. ball park mustard, such as
  French's
2 tbs. lime juice

¼ tsp. dried thyme
¼ tsp. dried sweet basil
½ tsp. allspice
¼ tsp. nutmeg
2 tsp. brown sugar
¼ tsp. freshly ground black pepper

Prepare chicken wings as described in *Chinese-Style Chicken Wings*, page 19. Place remaining ingredients in a mini-food chopper or blender and process until quite smooth. Pour over chicken wings and marinate in the refrigerator for at least 2 hours, or overnight. Remove from refrigerator about 30 minutes before grilling. Remove wings from marinade, drain and discard marinade. Grill for about 30 minutes, turning 3 to 4 times, until golden brown and thoroughly cooked.

BUFFALO-STYLE CHICKEN WINGS

Pieces: 20

*Grilling produces a very tasty, crisp and spicy chicken wing. This won't compete with the legendary deep fried version, but it is a little less calorific, and is delicious with the **Blue Cheese Dip**.*

10 chicken wings
2 tbs. vegetable oil

1 tbs. white wine vinegar
2 tbs. Crystal or Tabasco Sauce

Prepare chicken wings as described in *Chinese-Style Chicken Wings*, page 19. Combine oil, vinegar and hot sauce. Marinate wings in the refrigerator for at least 2 hours or overnight. Remove from marinade and cook on a preheated grill for about 30 minutes, turning 3 to 4 times, until golden brown and thoroughly cooked.

BLUE CHEESE DIP

This dip is also a great spread for toasted bread with the last of the red wine.

¼ cup blue cheese, crumbled
¼ cup sour cream

1 tsp. cider or wine vinegar
a few drops of hot sauce, to taste

Combine ingredients and thin with a little milk if needed.

TURKEY DIJON ROLL-UPS

These make a delicious party appetizer.

1 lb. package uncooked turkey breast slices, about ¼-inch thick
2 tbs. olive oil
2 tbs. Dijon mustard
8-10 thin stalks of asparagus, about ¼-inch diameter by 3 inches long
  or green beans, blanched for 2 minutes in boiling water
8-10 strips of red pepper, ¼-inch wide by 3 inches long
  or strips of carrot, blanched for 3 minutes in boiling water
salt and freshly ground pepper

Cut turkey slices in half to make 2 pieces about 3 inches square. Brush with olive oil and coat 1 side of each piece with mustard. Place 1 piece of asparagus or green bean and 1 strip of red pepper or carrot on mustard on each piece of meat. Roll up into a tight bundle and secure with a toothpick placed parallel to the meat seam. Cook on a preheated grill for about 3 to 4 minutes each side, turning once. Remove to a cutting board and allow to cool slightly. Trim the ends and cut each roll into 2 to 3 pieces. Cut on the diagonal so colors of vegetables show. Serve with *Thai-Style Dipping Sauce*, page 23.

THAI-STYLE DIPPING SAUCE

⅓ cup rice wine vinegar
⅓ cup sugar
dash salt and red pepper flakes
1 tbs. finely chopped cucumber, peeled and seeded
1 tbs. finely chopped fresh cilantro

Combine rice wine vinegar, sugar, salt and red pepper flakes in a small saucepan. Bring to a boil. Remove from heat, let cool, and add chopped cucumber and cilantro.

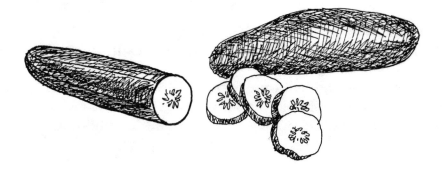

SHRIMP WITH SPICY MUSTARD SAUCE

Dip hot grilled shrimp into this piquant tarragon sauce for a terrific easy appetizer. Make the sauce a few hours or even a day ahead.

1/2 lb. medium shrimp, peeled, deveined
olive oil
salt and pepper

SAUCE

2 tbs. full-flavored olive oil
2 tbs. chicken stock
1 tbs. Dijon mustard
1 tbs. tarragon wine vinegar
1/4 tsp. dried tarragon

1 tbs. finely chopped parsley
1 small green onion, white part only,
    finely chopped
1/8 tsp. red pepper flakes, or to taste
salt and freshly ground pepper

Coat shrimp with oil and salt and pepper. Grill over high heat 5 to 6 minutes, turning once, or until shrimp are pink and firm to the touch. Do not overcook. Combine sauce ingredients in a small bowl, cover and refrigerate until ready to serve.

SHRIMP WITH SWEET HOT MUSTARD

This is a quick and easy shrimp treat.

½ lb. large shrimp, shelled, deveined
sweet hot mustard

Spread both sides of shrimp with a thin layer of sweet hot mustard. If shrimp are large, place on the preheated grill and cook for 3 to 4 minutes, or until shrimp turn pink and are firm to the touch. Place smaller shrimp on skewers for easy handling. Serve immediately.

VARIATION

Wrap mustard coated-shrimp with a thin strip of prosciutto or thinly sliced pastrami; then grill.

SESAME SHRIMP

These are wonderful for an informal party.

½ lb. large shrimp, shelled, deveined
3 tbs. soy sauce
1 clove garlic, finely minced
3 tsp. brown sugar
1 tsp. sesame oil
toasted sesame seeds

Combine soy sauce, garlic, brown sugar and sesame oil in a shallow dish. Marinate shrimp for 15 to 20 minutes. Arrange shrimp on presoaked wooden skewers or metal skewers and cook on a preheated grill for 3 to 4 minutes, or until shrimp turn pink and are firm to the touch. Sprinkle with sesame seeds and serve immediately.

VARIATION

Drain canned peeled water chestnuts and marinate 10 or 12 in soy sauce with shrimp. Alternate shrimp and water chestnuts on skewers and grill.

MIDDLE EASTERN CHICKEN STRIPS

Makes: 10-12 pieces

These are a delicious, low calorie appetizer and are good served in pita pockets with thinly sliced cucumbers and tomatoes. One of the ingredients, fenugreek, an aromatic plant from Asia or Southern Europe, has seeds which are pleasantly bitter, slightly sweet and can be used whole or ground.

1 lb. boneless, skinless chicken breasts

MARINADE

8 oz. plain yogurt
1/2 tsp. cumin
1/4 tsp. dry mustard
1/4 tsp. tumeric

1/8 tsp. cayenne pepper
1/4 tsp. fenugreek or curry powder
salt and freshly ground pepper

Slightly flatten chicken breasts between 2 sheets of waxed paper. Cut chicken breasts lengthwise into 1 1/2- to 2-inch wide strips. Thread each piece on 2 presoaked bamboo skewers placed about 3/4-inch apart. This keeps pieces flat while grilling. Combine marinade ingredients and pour over skewered chicken. Marinate about 30 minutes. Remove from marinade; cook on a preheated grill 1 to 2 minutes each side. Serve hot.

EGGPLANT AND HERBED GOAT CHEESE ROLLS

Makes: 12 pieces

Thin, bite-sized slices of eggplant are grilled and then filled with a savory goat cheese mixture. These are delicious at room temperature and go well with a crisp Sauvignon Blanc wine. Double the recipe to meet the demand.

1 small eggplant, about 3-4 inches
  diameter
olive oil
¼ cup fresh soft goat cheese or light
  cream cheese
1 tsp. minced fresh sweet basil
2 tsp. minced fresh Italian parsley

1 tsp. fresh minced chives
3 fresh sprigs thyme leaves
salt and generous amount of freshly
  ground pepper
3-4 full-flavored black olives, pitted,
  finely chopped or 1-2 sun-dried
  tomatoes, packed in oil, finely chopped

Cut 12 thin slices, about ⅛-inch thick, from eggplant. Brush both sides of eggplant with olive oil and grill for 5 to 6 minutes, turning frequently, until eggplant is soft and lightly browned. Remove from grill; allow to cool slightly. Combine remaining ingredients and place a teaspoonful of filling on each eggplant piece. Fold eggplant over to enclose filling or roll up into small rolls.

BREAD AND SAUSAGE SKEWERS
Makes: 5-6 skewers

Use substantial Italian or French bread, preferably a day or two old, and your favorite smoked or spicy-style sausage to make this satisfying appetizer.

2 sausages, about $\frac{1}{2}$ lb., Polish, Italian or your choice
$\frac{1}{3}$ cup dry white wine, apple juice or water
5-6 slices of bread about 1-inch thick, cut into $1\frac{1}{2}$-inch cubes
1 red or yellow bell pepper, seeded, cut into 1-inch squares
full-flavored olive oil

Precook raw sausages by steaming them covered in a small skillet with white wine, apple juice or water for about 10 minutes, or until sausages are no longer pink. Turn once or twice during cooking. Take off heat. When cool enough to handle, slice into $\frac{3}{4}$-inch thick slices. Alternate bread cubes, sausage and pepper pieces on presoaked wooden skewers or metal skewers. For heartier appetites, use longer skewers. Brush bread cubes and peppers with olive oil. Cook on preheated grill 2 to 3 minutes a side, or until bread and sausages are nicely browned. Serve hot.

SWISS CHARD BUNDLES

Swiss chard or sturdy lettuce leaves make excellent wrappers for savory grilled tidbits. Choose the smaller leaves and cut out the tougher thick stems after blanching. Any cheese is good but try full-flavored ones such as Gruyère, Kasseri, Manchego or smoked Gouda. These are great appetizers to do for a group.

For each bundle:

1 small Swiss chard, romaine or butter lettuce leaf
1 piece cheese about 1-inch square by $\frac{1}{4}$-inch thick
2-3 slivers oil cured sun-dried tomatoes
5-6 toasted pine nuts
olive oil for grilling

Bring a pot of water to a boil and blanch leaves for about 30 seconds. Remove from water and spread on paper towels to dry. Cut out any large stems that will be hard to fold. Place cheese in the center of leaf and top with sun-dried tomato slivers and pine nuts. Fold up sides of leaf, completely enclosing filling to make a small package. Brush both sides with olive oil. Grill over medium heat about 2 minutes a side, or until cheese seems soft to the touch. Serve warm.

BACON WRAPPED MUSHROOMS

Choose the thinnest sliced bacon you can find for this appetizer, or use a strip of pancetta.

12 mushrooms about 1¼-inch diameter
2 tbs. soy sauce
1 tsp. brown sugar
12 strips of bacon, about 4 inches long

Wash and trim mushrooms. Combine soy sauce and brown sugar in a small bowl and marinate mushrooms 10 to 15 minutes. Remove from marinade, wrap each with bacon and place on presoaked wooden skewers or metal skewers. Grill on a preheated grill about 12 to 14 minutes, or until bacon is crisp and brown. Turn frequently.

VARIATION

If you have some roasted garlic cloves on hand, wrap one in the bacon with each mushroom.

OYSTERS WITH MIGNONETTE SAUCE

Servings: 2-3

Grilled oysters in the shell are fun for an informal get-together. Clams and mussels are also good candidates for grilling.

12 oysters

Scrub shells. Place on a preheated grill with deeper side of shell down to keep most of oyster liquid with oyster. Grill about 8 to 10 minutes or until oysters start to sizzle and shells open slightly. Discard any oysters that do not open. Handle hot shells carefully and pry them open farther, if necessary, with an oyster or small bladed knife. Spoon on some Mignonette Sauce or a few drops of hot sauce or lemon, and enjoy.

MIGNONETTE SAUCE (FOR A DOZEN OYSTERS)

3 tbs. tarragon wine vinegar
3 tbs. dry white wine
1 tbs. finely minced shallot or
  2-3 green onions, finely chopped

$\frac{1}{2}$ small jalapeño pepper, seeded, finely chopped
$\frac{1}{2}$ tsp. grated lemon rind
salt and freshly ground white pepper

Combine ingredients and allow to stand an hour before serving so flavors have a chance to blend.

CROSTINI

Italian appetizer crostini or bruschetta toasts are easy to do on the grill. Cut bread into ½-inch thick slices.

1 crusty French loaf, approximately 15 inches long
1 clove garlic
olive oil
1 tomato, finely chopped
fresh basil leaves

Toast both sides of bread. Rub a cut clove of garlic over warm toast and drizzle on your best olive oil and a little fresh chopped garlic, or some fresh chopped tomatoes and sweet basil leaves. Toppings of prepared black olive paste, sun-dried tomatoes, or chopped chicken livers are other delicious choices. Serve with a chilled Pinot Grigio, Sauvignon Blanc or Sangiovese wine.

GRILLED MEATS

Meat is a popular choice for grilling when you want a hearty entrée. Ribs, burgers and steaks are palate pleasers, as are pork and lamb chops.

Marinades can be as simple as rubbing on a little olive oil and herbs, or some chile powder, or using a prepared barbecue sauce from the supermarket.

For general hints on grilling, see page 5. Here are a few specific tips for grilling meats:

- Be sure to cook ground beef to 150°, and pork products to 165°, to destroy any harmful bacteria or parasites.

- Refrigerate meat if marinating for longer than 2 hours.

- Trim steaks and chops well; otherwise the fat will drip onto the grill coils, causing excessive smoking and possibility of flareups.

- Choose thinly cut (less than 1 inch) steaks and chops for faster cooking. Most indoor grills do not put out enough heat to perfectly cook 2-inch steaks.

- Cut meat in no larger than 1-1½-inch uniformly sized pieces for kabobs or skewers. Use two parallel or double skewers to keep meat in place when turning on the grill.

THAI BEEF SATAY

Serve with rice, a fruit salad or cooked snow peas.

1 small flank steak, about 1½ lb.

MARINADE

1 tsp. finely minced garlic
1 tsp. grated fresh ginger
1 can (14½ oz.) coconut milk
1 tbs. soy sauce
1 tsp. curry powder
1 tsp. tumeric

Trim flank steak of all surface fat and silver skin. Place in the freezer for 20 minutes to firm meat for slicing. Cut at an angle, across grain, making strips about 1 inch wide and ⅛-inch thick. You will have about 20 strips. Combine marinade ingredients and marinate meat for about 30 minutes. Thread strips of meat on presoaked wooden skewers. Pour remaining marinade into a small saucepan.

Add:

2 tbs. sugar
a pinch cayenne pepper
a pinch ground cloves
a pinch black pepper
a pinch ground cinnamon
a pinch cumin
1 tsp. paprika
generous dash of Tabasco Sauce

1 tbs. creamy peanut butter

Bring to a boil over medium heat and simmer for a few minutes. Remove from heat and stir in peanut butter.

When the grill is hot, grill strips for about 2 minutes on each side. The meat will cook quickly. Serve sauce in a shallow dish. Dip hot beef satay in sauce before eating.

MOROCCAN-STYLE KEFTA

These flavorful ground meat rolls are grilled and sold by street vendors in Morocco. Slip the grilled meats into pita pocket breads and serve with a yogurt cucumber sauce. Form the rolls on skewers ahead of time and refrigerate; when they are well chilled, they are less likely to come apart on the grill during cooking.

2 green onions, white part only
1 large clove garlic
1/4 cup Italian parsley leaves
1/2 tsp. cumin
1/2 tsp. paprika

1/4 tsp. Tabasco Sauce
1 tsp. salt
1/2 lb. ground lamb
1/2 lb. ground chuck
juice of 1 lemon

Place onion, garlic, parsley, cumin, paprika, Tabasco and salt in a food processor bowl. Pulse several times to finely mince, scraping down sides of bowl once or twice. Add lamb, beef and lemon juice. Pulse 2 to 3 times to combine ingredients. Divide mixture into 8 equal-sized pieces and form into balls. Poke a skewer through center of each ball. Moisten hands with water and stretch meat into a sausage shape on the skewer, about 1 inch in diameter and 3 to 4 inches long. Cover and refrigerate for at least 1 hour before grilling.

Spray grill with nonstick cooking spray. When grill is hot, place skewered meat on rack and turn every few minutes until sausages are cooked through, about 12 to 15 minutes. Remove from grill, slide off skewers, and serve in warmed pita pockets with *Yogurt Cucumber Sauce.*

YOGURT CUCUMBER SAUCE

1 cup lowfat plain yogurt
3 green onions, finely chopped
1 tsp. dried dill
1 tbs. rice wine vinegar
1 medium cucumber, peeled, seeded,
  coarsely grated, about 1 cup
1 medium tomato, peeled, seeded, chopped
salt and freshly ground pepper

Combine all ingredients and pour into a serving bowl. Refrigerate for at least an hour before serving. Spoon sauce into pita pockets with Kefta or serve on the side.

BLUE CHEESE STUFFED BURGERS

These zesty hamburgers have a moist blue cheese stuffing. Serve on toasted buns with a trio of vegetable salads on the side.

1 lb. lean ground beef
3 tbs. blue cheese crumbles
2 tsp. Worcestershire sauce
¼ tsp. garlic salt
dash Tabasco Sauce

Form meat into 8 equal-sized thin patties. Combine remaining ingredients in a small bowl, mixing well. Spread ¼ of cheese mixture on each of 4 patties, stopping about ¼ inch from edge of meat. Press remaining patties over filling, crimping edges to seal filling inside. Grill on a preheated grill about 5 minutes each side, or until cooked to taste. Serve immediately.

SUPER BURGERS

Here is a delicious variation for grilled hamburgers. Toast the buns on the grill, too. Make a side dish of oven fries by cutting unpeeled baking potatoes into 8 or 10 wedges. Brush with full-flavored olive oil, sprinkle with salt and pepper, and bake in a 425° oven about 30 minutes until brown and crisp.

1 lb. lean ground beef
3 tbs. finely chopped onion
1 tbs. Worcestershire sauce
salt and freshly ground pepper

Lightly mix ingredients and form into ½- to ¾-inch thick patties. Grill on a preheated grill about 4 minutes a side, or to desired doneness. Serve immediately.

ISLAND MARINATED STEAKS

Servings: 4

This marinade flavored with rum and lime juice is great for beef or chicken. Use bourbon or brandy for a new taste.

4 skirt steaks or market steaks about ¾-inch thick
2 tbs. rum
1 tbs. soy sauce
1 tbs. lime juice
1 tbs. brown sugar
1 tbs. Dijon mustard
1 tsp. Worcestershire sauce
1 tsp. vegetable oil
1 clove garlic, minced
2 tbs. finely chopped onion

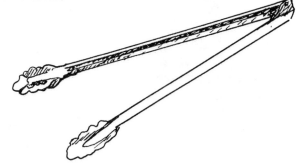

Combine ingredients and pour over steaks. Marinate for at least 30 minutes at room temperature or overnight in the refrigerator. Remove from refrigerator about 30 minutes before grilling. Preheat the grill and cook steaks about 6 minutes each side, depending on thickness and personal preference.

BEEF GYRO-STYLE

Flank steak strips are marinated in a Middle Eastern-style dressing and grilled.

1 lb. flank steak or top round sirloin, trimmed, cut into ⅛-inch side strips across
  the grain
4-5 pita breads, cut in half
lettuce, tomato, cucumber for garnish
1-1½ cups yogurt

MARINADE

2 tbs. vegetable oil
⅓ cup dry red wine
1 large clove garlic, minced
¼ tsp. dried oregano

¼ tsp. dried mint leaves, or 5-6 fresh
  mint leaves finely chopped
salt and freshly ground pepper

Combine marinade ingredients and pour over meat. Marinate for at least 30 minutes before grilling. Cook on a hot preheated grill 2 to 3 minutes each side.

To serve, arrange lettuce pieces on a platter with peeled, seeded, chopped tomatoes and thin cucumber slices. Fill pita breads with hot grilled meat and salad mixture; top with a spoonful of plain yogurt.

FLANK STEAK

Flank steak makes a delicious quick dinner entrée. Leftovers are great for sandwiches.

flank steak, trimmed, about 1½ lb.

MARINADE

2 tbs. vegetable oil
grated lemon rind from 1 lemon
2 tbs. lemon juice
2 tbs. soy sauce
1 quarter-sized piece fresh ginger, finely chopped
1 clove garlic, minced
1 tsp. brown sugar

Combine marinade ingredients and pour over meat. Marinate for about 30 minutes before grilling. Drain meat and cook on a preheated grill about 4 to 5 minutes each side for medium rare meat. Remove meat to a cutting board and cut into thin slices diagonally across the grain. Serve immediately.

KOREAN BEEF

Servings: 2-3

This is our version of one of Korea's national dishes, Bul-Kogi.

1 lb. flank steak
toasted sesame seeds for garnish

MARINADE

¼ cup soy sauce
¼ cup beef or chicken stock
2-3 green onions, white part only, cut
  into ½-inch pieces
1 quarter-sized piece of fresh ginger,
  peeled, diced

3 large cloves garlic, peeled, diced
2 tbs. sugar
1 tbs. sesame seed oil
white pepper

Trim flank steak and place in the freezer for about 30 minutes. Combine marinade ingredients in a blender or mini-chopper and process until smooth. With a sharp knife, cut flank steak across grain, diagonally, into strips ¼-inch thick by 1 inch wide, approximately 4 to 5 inches long. Hold the knife at an angle to make nice wide pieces. Pour marinade over strips and let stand at room temperature about 20 minutes, stirring meat mixture once or twice. Grill on a preheated grill 1 to 2 minutes a side until meat is nicely browned. Sprinkle with sesame seeds and serve immediately.

FENNEL-FLAVORED PORK KABOBS

Servings: 2-3

Fennel or anise flavors marry well with pork. Alternate pork pieces with partially cooked small new potatoes or carrot chunks and serve a crisp green salad or vegetable for an easy dinner.

1 pork tenderloin, trimmed, about 10-12 oz.
1 tsp. fennel seed, ground
1 tbs. olive oil
1 tsp. lemon juice
salt and freshly ground pepper

OPTIONAL

8 small new potatoes parboiled or partially cooked in the microwave
2-3 carrots, peeled, cut into 1-inch pieces, partially cooked

Cut pork tenderloin into ¾-inch-thick chunks. Combine fennel seeds, olive oil, lemon juice, salt and pepper. Rub mixture into meat and allow to marinate about 30 minutes before grilling. Thread meat on presoaked wooden skewers or metal skewers with potatoes and/or carrots, if desired. Grill on a preheated grill about 15 to 18 minutes, turning 2 or 3 times, until meat is firm to the touch and no longer pink, with an internal temperature of 165°.

BABY BACK RIBS

Servings: 2-3

These ribs are precooked in the oven and then marinated. This cuts the grilling time considerably and allows the ribs to remain juicy and flavorful. You can do the baking and marinating the day before. Wrap a whole head of garlic sprinkled with a little olive oil in foil and bake it along with the meat. Squeeze the soft cooked garlic from the cloves to make a wonderful spread for hot grilled bread to serve with the ribs. The marinade can be doubled if you want to do a larger quantity.

1¼-1½ lb. rack of pork baby back ribs
2 cloves garlic, peeled and smashed
¼ cup soy sauce

2 tbs. hoisin sauce
1 tsp. fresh grated ginger
2 tbs. white wine vinegar

Preheat oven to 350°. Wrap ribs in foil with 2 cloves of garlic. Bake for 45 minutes. Combine remaining ingredients and pour over hot ribs along with meat juices. Cool for a few minutes and then refrigerate for 2 to 3 hours or overnight. Remove from refrigerator about 30 minutes before grilling. Drain ribs, place on a preheated grill and cook for 10 to 12 minutes, turning frequently and brushing with marinade. Serve hot.

APPLE GLAZED BABY BACK RIBS

*Apples and pork are a classic combination. This light fruity marinade lets the succulent pork flavor come through. Serve this with **Confetti Coleslaw**, page 118, and some **Toasty Yukon Gold Potatoes**, page 138. There will be some of the sauce made from the marinade left over for the potatoes.*

2 racks baby back ribs (about 1 lb. each)
2 cups apple cider or apple juice
2 tbs. soy sauce
3 cloves garlic, thinly sliced
2 tsp. Dijon mustard
2 tbs. apple cider vinegar
white pepper

Place ribs in a 9 x 13 pan, bone side down. Add apple juice, soy sauce and garlic. Cover tightly with aluminum foil and place in a 350° oven. Bake for 45 minutes. Remove from oven, discard garlic and strain pan juices into a small saucepan. Heat over high heat and reduce volume to about half. Remove from heat; stir in mustard and apple cider vinegar. Add a pinch of white pepper. Preheat grill. When hot, brush racks of ribs with sauce and grill 10 to 12 minutes, turning frequently. When hot and nicely glazed, remove from grill and cut into serving-sized pieces. Serve hot.

PLUM GLAZED SPARERIBS

This recipe works well with either baby back ribs or St. Louis cut spareribs. The ribs are precooked in the oven and finished on the grill. There is enough marinade to make a double batch of ribs. Cook two racks and hold in a 300° oven while the last racks are grilling. Both the Chinese plum sauce and chile paste with garlic are available in most supermarkets in the Asian foods section.

2 racks of spareribs, about 1¼ lb. each
⅓ cup water

1 clove garlic, thinly sliced
5-6 thin slices fresh ginger

MARINADE

⅓ cup Chinese plum sauce
3 tbs. soy sauce
2 tbs. honey

2 tbs. rice wine vinegar
½ tsp. chile paste with garlic

Place spareribs and water in a 9 x 13 pan; sprinkle meat with garlic and ginger slices. Cover pan with aluminum foil and bake ribs in a 350° oven for 1 hour. Combine marinade ingredients. Preheat grill, drain spareribs and place racks of ribs on grill. Brush with marinade. Grill 12 to 15 minutes; turning frequently until meat is nicely browned. Brush with marinade each time ribs are turned. Serve hot.

QUICK GRILLED PORK CHOPS

Servings: 2

Thinly cut pork chops make a quick grilled dinner. Here are several marinade variations. Be sure to cook the pork until it reaches an internal temperature of 165°.

1 lb. thinly cut pork chops, about ½-inch thick

MARINADE #1

Trim off fat and sprinkle both sides of chops with prepared seasoned salt. Grill for 5 to 6 minutes each side, turning once.

MARINADE #2

Brush with olive oil and a few drops of lemon juice. Rub in 1 finely minced clove of garlic and some fresh thyme leaves. Grill as above.

MARINADE #3

Brush with olive oil and a few drops of lemon juice. Grill and sprinkle each chop with a few drops of good balsamic vinegar.

YOGURT MARINATED PORK CHOPS

Servings: 2

*A mini-chopper or food processor makes this a quick marinade. Choose thinly cut pork chops, about ¾-inch thick for fast grilling. Serve with **South American Salsa**, page 52, or a spicy chutney and hot tortillas on the side.*

1 lb. thinly cut pork chops
1 large garlic clove
2 green onions, white part only
1 quarter-sized piece peeled
  fresh ginger
¼ cup cilantro leaves

½ small jalapeño pepper or to taste
1 tsp. lemon juice
½ cup plain yogurt
1 tsp. cumin
salt and freshly ground pepper

Trim fat off pork chops and place on a shallow plate. Coarsely chop garlic, green onions, ginger, cilantro leaves and hot pepper in a mini-chopper or food processor. Add remaining ingredients and process until smooth. Pour over pork chops and marinate about 30 minutes. Grill over high heat about 5 to 6 minutes per side until meat is firm to the touch, and has reached an internal temperature of 165°.

SOUTH AMERICAN SALSA

Makes: 2 cups

This is similar to the Mexican Mantequilla de Pobre, or poor man's butter, with some extra zip. It can be made a day ahead and refrigerated. If there is any left over, tuck some into a hot tortilla with scrambed eggs, or spread it on crackers for a quick appetizer.

1 medium avocado, peeled, seeded, diced
1 large tomato, peeled, seeded, diced
1 small jalapeño pepper, seeded, minced
2 tbs. finely chopped red or green bell pepper
1 small clove garlic, finely minced
1 hard cooked egg, peeled, finely chopped

2 tbs. finely chopped parsley
2 tbs. finely chopped fresh cilantro
¼ tsp. dried oregano
1 tbs. full-flavored olive oil
1 tbs. white wine vinegar
1 tsp. lemon juice
½ tsp. Dijon mustard
salt and freshly ground pepper

Combine avocado, tomato, peppers, garlic, egg, parsley, cilantro and oregano in a glass or stainless steel bowl. Mix olive oil with remaining ingredients and pour over avocado mixture. Toss to combine. Cover and allow to marinate for about 30 minutes.

SMOKY PORK CHOPS

A few drops of Liquid Smoke add an extra flavor dimension to this marinade. Use a mini-chopper for easy blending. **Confetti Coleslaw**, *page 118, or* **Quick Mexican Bean Salad**, *page 122, and some corn bread make a wonderful combination.*

1 lb. thinly cut pork chops, about ½-inch thick

MARINADE

1 tbs. lime juice
1 tbs. apple juice
1 tbs. vegetable oil
1 large clove garlic, minced
¼ tsp. paprika
3-4 drops Liquid Smoke
salt and freshly ground pepper

Combine marinade ingredients and brush on both sides of chops. Marinate for about 30 minutes. Grill on a preheated grill 12 to 14 minutes, or until pork reaches 165°. Turn once during grilling. Serve immediately.

THYME LAMB CHOPS

Servings: 3-4

Choose lamb chops no more than ¾-inch thick for even grilling. Serve with grilled new potatoes and a bright green vegetable. These are good with fresh minced rosemary or oregano instead of thyme.

12 rib lamb chops, about ¾-inch thick
1 tbs. full-flavored olive oil
1 tbs. lemon juice
1 tbs. fresh thyme leaves, minced
salt and freshly ground pepper

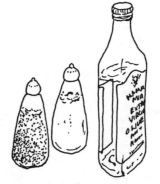

Trim all exterior fat from lamb chops, coat both sides with olive oil and press some thyme leaves into both sides of meat. Sprinkle with lemon juice, salt and pepper. Marinate at room temperature for about 30 minutes. Cook on a preheated grill about 5 minutes a side, until medium rare, or to taste. Serve immediately on heated plates.

TURKISH-STYLE LAMB

*This fragrant marinade features yogurt and fresh herbs. After grilling, serve the lamb with **Yogurt Cucumber Sauce**, page 39, couscous and fresh pita breads.*

1 lb. leg of lamb, trimmed and cut into ¾-inch cubes

MARINADE

2 tbs. full-flavored olive oil
¼ cup plain yogurt
1 tbs. lemon juice
2 tbs. chopped onion
1-2 sprigs fresh thyme
1 tsp. chopped fresh mint leaves
1 tbs. fresh cilantro leaves
salt and freshly ground pepper

Combine marinade ingredients in a mini-chopper or blender and process until smooth. Pour over lamb. Marinate at least 30 minutes before grilling. Thread lamb on presoaked wooden skewers or metal skewers and cook on a hot grill 12 to 15 minutes, turning once or twice during grilling. Serve hot.

LAMB SHISH KABOBS

Servings: 4

Here is a flavorful, spicy marinade for leg of lamb. Alternate green or red pepper squares and onion pieces between the meat cubes for extra flavor and color. Serve with hot garlic bread, fresh cooked ears of corn and sliced tomatoes.

1 lb. leg of lamb, trimmed and cut into 3/4-inch cubes

MARINADE

1/4 cup chopped onions
1/2-inch square piece fresh ginger root, chopped
1 large clove garlic, chopped
2 tbs. lemon juice
2 tbs. full-flavored olive oil
1 tsp. cumin

1 tbs. fresh chopped parsley
1/2 tsp. dried mint or 6-8 fresh leaves, chopped
1/2 small jalapeño chile pepper, or to taste
pinch cinnamon
salt and freshly ground pepper

Combine marinade ingredients in a mini-food chopper or blender and process until smooth. Pour over lamb pieces and marinate for at least 30 minutes before grilling. Place lamb on presoaked wood or metal skewers and grill on a hot grill for 12 to 15 minutes, turning once or twice during cooking. Serve immediately.

MARINATED LAMB

*This is a zesty marinade that can be done the night before. Use a double plastic bag for easy turning and cleanup. Serve with **Rice Stuffed Tomatoes**, page 124, and a crisp green vegetable.*

1 lb. leg of lamb, trimmed and cut into ³⁄₄-inch pieces

MARINADE

3 tbs. olive oil
1 tbs. lemon juice
1 tbs. red wine vinegar
2 tbs. finely chopped onion
1 large clove garlic, minced
½ tsp. Dijon mustard

½ tsp. dried oregano
½ tsp. dried sweet basil
2 tbs. finely chopped Italian parsley
dash red pepper flakes
freshly ground pepper

Place lamb in a plastic bag or glass dish. Combine marinade ingredients and pour over meat. Refrigerate 4 hours or overnight, turning lamb once or twice to distribute marinade. Remove from refrigerator about 30 minutes before grilling. Drain lamb and arrange on presoaked wooden skewers or metal skewers. Cook on a preheated grill about 12 to 15 minutes, turning 2 or 3 times during cooking.

GRILLED SEAFOOD

Succulent pink shrimp, skewers of scallops and golden salmon steaks immediately come to mind when thinking about grilled seafood. Fish is one of the easiest things to grill because of its quick cooking time. You can tell when it is done because it either changes color or translucency, and the texture becomes firm to the touch or flakes easily.

A few helpful tips:

- Always spray the grill with nonstick cooking spray before grilling. This makes it easier to turn the fish over and makes cleanup after grilling less difficult.
- Cook seafood on the highest grill setting, and be sure to preheat the grill. Fragile, thin fish fillets can be grilled on fresh lettuce leaves or canned grape leaves for easier turning.
- Use two parallel skewers or double skewers for scallops and oysters for better control when turning them over.
- Seafood only needs a short time to marinate. Marinades with a lot of lemon juice tend to "cook" the fish, resulting in a mushy texture.
- A grill rack with small mesh is useful for cooking small shrimp, scallops and fragile fish. It can be placed over the regular rack.

- Grill size generally limits the number of portions, depending on the dimensions of the fish. Skewers of seafood can be done in several batches if you want to serve several people, and the skewers can easily be prepared and refrigerated ahead of time for a party.
- If you are using one of the hinged grills, the fish will cook in considerably less time than suggested in the recipe. Use the manufacturer's recommended timing for the specific type of fish.

Fresh seafood, hot off the grill, is marvelous. Party fare includes some elegant *Salmon Pinwheels* and a savory paella. Try the *Scallop, Avocado and Walnut Salad* for a delicious first course for your next dinner party. When you want to splurge, *Lobster Tails with Garlic Butter* make a very special dinner for two.

This section includes many quick and easy marinades and sauces for those days you need a fast dinner. Consider serving fresh grilled seafood on a bed of creamy spinach or chopped leeks sautéed in a little butter, or some garlic mashed potatoes. Your favorite fish can be easily substituted in any of these recipes. Give yourself a treat and get in the grilled seafood habit!

HALIBUT WITH CHARMOULA MARINADE

This Moroccan marinade is marvelous for grilling halibut, swordfish, shrimp, scallops, chicken breasts or turkey scallops. Serve with **Toasty Yukon Potatoes,** *page 138, or* **Polenta**, *page 127. If there is a little marinade left over, spoon it over the cooked fish.*

1-1¼ lb. halibut, about ¾-inch thick

⅓ cup full-flavored olive oil
3 tbs. lemon juice
2 cloves garlic, minced
2 tbs. minced fresh parsley

2 tbs. minced fresh cilantro leaves
3-4 fresh mint leaves, finely chopped
½ tsp. paprika
1 tsp. cumin
dash Tabasco Sauce
salt and freshly ground pepper

Combine all ingredients and pour over fish. Marinate for 10 to 15 minutes and place on a preheated grill. Cook about 6 to 7 minutes each side over high heat, until fish is opaque and firm to the touch.

VARIATION

Substitute 1 lb. thinly sliced turkey breast for halibut.

HERBED SCALLOPS

Scallops and tarragon are a classic combination and this marinade goes together quickly. Remember to soak bamboo skewers for about 15 minutes before using on the grill and use 2 parallel skewers to keep the scallops from rolling when turning. This can be served as an appetizer or entrée; just double the recipe amounts as needed. Serve with a rice pilaf, fresh garden peas, grilled garlic bread and a nice crisp Sauvignon Blanc or Chardonnay for a delicious summer dinner.

½ lb. scallops, about 1-inch diameter
1 tsp. fresh tarragon, finely chopped
4 tbs. butter, melted
2 tbs. white wine or lemon juice
salt and freshly ground pepper
4-5 green onions, cut into 1-inch pieces

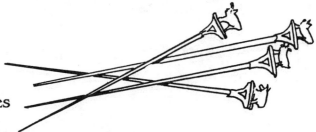

Combine tarragon, butter, white wine, salt and pepper. Toss scallops in butter mixture and thread onto small bamboo skewers, 3 to 4 per skewer. Alternate scallops on skewers with pieces of green onion. Preheat grill and cook for 3 to 4 minutes each side, turning once. Serve immediately.

LEMON THYME SCALLOPS

Scallops are marinated in lemon juice, olive oil and fresh thyme and then grilled. While the grill is hot, cook some eggplant or zucchini and sweet onion slices before cooking the scallops. Some grilled garlic bread would be a great accompaniment.

$\frac{1}{2}$ lb. large sea scallops
grated rind from 1 lemon
2 tbs. lemon juice
2 tbs. full-flavored olive oil
1 tsp. fresh thyme leaves, finely chopped
salt and freshly ground pepper

Grate lemon rind and set aside. Combine remaining ingredients in a shallow bowl. Carefully wash scallops, remove the tough muscle from the side, and rinse well. Marinate scallops in lemon/olive oil mixture for 10 to 15 minutes. Preheat the grill and place scallops on grilling rack. Cook for about 6 minutes each side, depending on grill temperature, or until scallops are firm to the touch. Place scallops on warm plates and sprinkle with grated lemon rind. Serve immediately.

SCALLOP, AVOCADO AND WALNUT SALAD

Servings: 4 as appetizer
or 2 as main course

Hot grilled scallops fill the center of a plate of tender greens and avocado pieces, accented with crunchy toasted walnuts. This is an elegant first course or a great luncheon salad. The scallops are easy to handle if you grill them on parallel presoaked skewers. Make salad first and then grill scallops.

12 oz. small sea scallops, about 1-inch diameter
1 tbs. light olive oil
1 tbs. lemon juice

Carefully wash scallops, remove small tough muscle on side and rinse well. Combine oil and lemon juice and marinate scallops in mixture about 10 minutes. Thread on 3 to 4 skewers and grill on a preheated grill about 5 minutes each side, or until firm. Do not overcook.

butter lettuce leaves
baby spinach leaves
1 tbs. light olive oil
1 tbs. walnut oil
1 tbs. sherry wine vinegar
salt and freshly ground pepper

1 ripe avocado, peeled, cut into
  3/4- inch pieces
1/2 cup toasted chopped walnuts
1-2 tbs. grated Parmesan cheese, optional

Tear butter lettuce into bite-sized pieces and combine with spinach. Combine oils, sherry vinegar, salt and pepper; toss with salad greens. Arrange salad greens around the edge of individual salad plates and scatter avocado and walnut pieces over greens. Place cooked scallops in center of greens, sprinkle with Parmesan cheese and serve immediately.

GREEK SHRIMP SALAD

Hot grilled shrimp are served on the same platter with a zesty Greek salad with cucumbers, tomatoes, olives and feta cheese for a great summer dinner or patio luncheon. Serve with some good French bread to mop up the juices. This salad is also a good accompaniment for many grilled meats.

1/2 lb. medium shrimp, peeled, deveined
1 tbs. olive oil
1 tbs. lemon juice
dash red pepper flakes

SALAD

1/2 head iceberg lettuce, torn into bite-
   sized pieces
1 small cucumber, peeled, seeded,
   thinly sliced
1/2 small red onion, thinly sliced
1/2 small red or green bell pepper,
   peeled, thinly sliced

2 small ripe tomatoes, peeled, seeded,
   diced
2 oz. feta cheese, coarsely crumbled
8-10 Kalamata olives
5-6 marinated artichoke hearts

DRESSING

1/4 cup full-flavored olive oil
1/2 tsp. dried basil, or 1 tbs. minced fresh basil
1 tsp. dried oregano
2 tbs. red wine vinegar
1 clove garlic
1 tbs. feta cheese
salt and freshly ground pepper

Marinate peeled shrimp with olive oil, lemon juice and red pepper flakes for 10 to 15 minutes. Thread on metal or presoaked wooden skewers for easy turning. Time grilling so salad is made and ready to serve. When the grill is hot, cook shrimp about 3 to 4 minutes per side, depending on temperature of grill. The shrimp should be pink and firm to the touch. Do not overcook.

Place salad ingredients in a medium bowl. Combine dressing ingredients in a mini-chopper. Process until ingredients are smooth and well combined. Pour over salad and toss to combine. Distribute salad onto individual plates, leaving room for shrimp. Arrange grilled shrimp beside salad. Serve immediately.

FRESH BASIL SHRIMP

Choose medium to large shrimp for ease of shelling and cooking. The fresh basil leaves are an attractive and flavorful foil for the shrimp. Serve as an appetizer or entrée, doubling the recipe as required.

1/2 lb. medium to large shrimp, shelled, deveined

3 tbs. melted butter
1/2 tsp. minced fresh garlic
dash Tabasco Sauce

1 tsp. lemon juice
salt and freshly ground pepper
1 bunch fresh sweet basil

Combine butter, garlic, Tabasco, lemon juice, salt and pepper. Toss peeled shrimp in butter. Wrap shrimp in large basil leaves and thread onto skewers, alternating shrimp with smaller basil leaves. Use 2 parallel skewers for threading shrimp so they can be easily turned on the grill. Brush shrimp with remaining butter mixture and grill on high heat for about 2 to 3 minutes per side, or until shrimp turn pink and feel firm to the touch. Baste with more butter before turning shrimp. Serve immediately.

SOLE ON LETTUCE LEAVES

Servings: 2

The lettuce leaves should be slightly larger than the fillets.

3 or 4 small pieces of sole or other thin
  fish fillets
6 or 8 romaine or butter lettuce leaves

salt and white pepper
minced parsley for garnish

SHALLOT SAUCE

1 tbs. minced shallot
½ cup dry white wine or vermouth

3 tbs. butter
salt and freshly ground pepper

Season fish with salt and pepper. Arrange each piece on a lettuce leaf skin side up. Place fish on leaves on a preheated grill and grill about 4 minutes. Place second lettuce leaf on top, turn fish over, remove cooked lettuce leaf and continue to grill 3 to 4 minutes. Cook minced shallot and white wine together in a small saucepan until all but about a tablespoon of wine has evaporated. Over very low heat gradually stir in butter a little at a time; add some salt and pepper. Serve fish on bottom lettuce leaf and spoon some butter sauce over each portion. Sprinkle with parsley and serve immediately.

TROUT AMANDINE

Fresh trout is widely available in fish markets today, and is particularly good grilled. If you can, get boneless trout, or ask your fish merchant to bone them for you. They are a snap to grill and serve. Make the almond butter sauce while the trout are cooking. A little rice or couscous would make a delicious accompaniment.

2 boneless trout, skin on, 10 oz. each, before boning
olive oil

Spray the grill with nonstick cooking spray and preheat. Open trout so they are flat and brush both sides with olive oil. When grill is hot, place on rack starting with skin side down. Grill about 3 minutes each side, depending on hotness of grill. Trout is done when it turns opaque and is firm to the touch. Remove skin and place on individual serving plates. Top with *Amandine Sauce.*

Whole trout can be grilled without removing bones. Grill about 7 minutes per side.

AMANDINE SAUCE

3 tbs. butter
4 tbs. slivered almonds
2 tsp. lemon juice

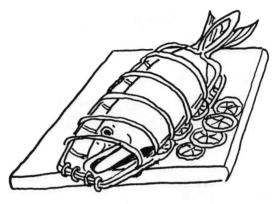

Melt butter and sauté almonds in butter for 3 to 4 minutes until almonds are lightly browned. Stir in lemon juice and pour over trout. Serve immediately.

MEXICAN-STYLE SEAFOOD SALAD

Servings: 2

This salad has the fresh flavors of seviche. Grilled sea bass or halibut is marinated and served with fresh avocado, tomatoes and cilantro for a delicious warm weather first course or a picnic dish. Do this ahead so it can marinate for at least an hour in the refrigerator before serving.

1 lb. sea bass or other firm-fleshed fish
  fillet
olive oil
1 smail red bell pepper
2 tbs. fresh lemon juice
2 tbs. fresh lime juice
1 tbs. light olive oil
1/2 fresh jalapeño pepper or to taste,
  seeds removed, finely minced
3 green onions, finely chopped

1/2 tsp. dried oregano
1/2 tsp. hot pepper sauce or Tabasco Sauce
salt and freshly ground pepper
1 large avocado, peeled, diced
2 large tomatoes, peeled, seeded,
  diced
1 head butter lettuce, torn into bite-
  sized pieces
fresh cilantro for garnish

When the grill is hot, brush fish with oil and grill for 10 to 12 minutes until firm to the touch. Remove to a plate and allow to cool. Roast red pepper on grill until all sides are charred. Place under a small bowl or in a plastic bag to steam for at least 15 minutes. Remove skin and seeds and cut ½ of pepper into ¼-inch dice. Reserve other half for another use.

Cut fish into ¾-inch cubes and combine with lemon and lime juice, olive oil, jalapeño pepper, green onions, oregano, hot sauce, salt and pepper. Cover and refrigerate to marinate for at least 1 hour. When ready to serve, toss fish with avocado, tomatoes and red pepper. Arrange lettuce on individual salad plates or a platter, top with fish and vegetables and garnish generously with cilantro leaves. Crisp corn chips or hot tortillas are a good accompaniment.

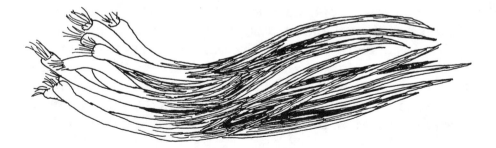

SALMON PINWHEELS

*These are easy to eat and can be prepared ahead of time. Marinate and grill them just before dinner. A nice crisp Chardonnay, **Rice Pilaf,** page 123, and some fresh asparagus would make an excellent combination.*

4 salmon steaks about ¾-inch thick
olive oil
lemon juice for marinating
1 tbs. melted butter
1 tbs. lemon juice

⅛ tsp. dried dill weed or ¼ tsp. dried
  tarragon
salt and freshly ground pepper

Remove skin and carefully cut down along the center bone, freeing salmon strips. Starting at the narrow tip of each strip, gently form strip into a pinwheel shape. Use a toothpick through the middle of each piece to keep the pinwheel from unwinding. Brush both sides of pinwheels with olive oil, salt and pepper, and sprinkle with a few drops of lemon juice. Marinate for about 10 minutes. When the grill is hot, cook for about 4 to 5 minutes each side until fish is firm to the touch. Do not overcook. Pull out toothpicks or warn your guests. Combine melted butter, lemon juice, dill, salt and pepper. Pour over salmon pinwheels and serve immediately.

SALMON CAKES

Here are the familiar canned salmon patties done on the grill. They are brown and crusty on the outside and contain considerably less fat than the traditional frying pan version. Serve with a creamed vegetable or your favorite tartar sauce.

1 can (15 ozs.) pink salmon, drained
1 egg
$\frac{1}{4}$ cup medium fine cracker crumbs
2-3 tbs. chopped fresh cilantro
dash Tabasco Sauce
salt and freshly ground pepper
vegetable oil for grilling

Pick over salmon, discarding skin and bones, and flake with a fork. Add remaining ingredients and shape into 4 patties about $\frac{3}{4}$-inch thick. Brush each side with vegetable oil and grill on a preheated grill about 7 to 8 minutes each side, or until lightly browned and firm to the touch. Serve immediately.

SALMON IN GRAPE LEAVES

Servings: 4

Wrapping fish in grape leaves for grilling adds a delicious flavor and keeps the fish moist. Cut the stem from the grape leaf, rinse in cold water and pat dry before wrapping the fish. Lay 2 or 3 grape leaves slightly overlapping so the salmon can be completely encased. Trout and halibut are also good candidates for this technique.

2 oz. salmon fillets, 6-7 oz. each
olive oil
salt and pepper
$\frac{1}{2}$ tsp. dried tarragon or 2 sprigs fresh
6-8 canned grape leaves

Lightly brush salmon with olive oil, season with salt and pepper and sprinkle with tarragon. Place each fillet on overlapped grape leaves, bringing up sides to completely enclose fish. Brush grape leaf packets with olive oil. Grill over high heat on a preheated grill 6 to 7 minutes each side, turning once. Serve in leaves and pass *Lemon and Olive Oil Dressing*, page 77.

LEMON AND OLIVE OIL DRESSING FOR FISH

2 tbs. olive oil
1 tbs. lemon juice
salt and freshly ground pepper
1 tbs. chopped parsley

Combine ingredients and serve as a light sauce for any grilled fish.

SEAFOOD PAELLA

A savory rice mixture is topped with hot grilled shrimp, scallops or other seafood. Clams in the shell can be grilled and added as well. Another delicious variation would be to add grilled chunks of chicken and spicy sausage. Be sure to use short grain rice in this dish. Make the skewers of seafood ahead of time and grill them just as the rice is about to be done.

2 tbs. full-flavored olive oil
1 large onion, finely chopped
2 large cloves garlic, finely chopped
1 red or 1 green bell pepper, coarsely
  chopped
1½ cups short grained rice
3 cups chicken stock, heated to boiling
1 tbs. lemon juice

1 large tomato, peeled, seeded,
  chopped
pinch saffron
5-6 drops Tabasco Sauce, or to taste
½ cup defrosted, frozen green peas
2-3 tbs. finely chopped parsley
salt and freshly ground pepper

8-10 clams in the shell, optional
12 medium shrimp, peeled, deveined
12 small scallops

olive oil and a few drops of lemon juice
  to brush on seafood
1 large chorizo sausage
⅓ cup white wine or water

Heat olive oil in a large skillet or deep sauté pan. Over low heat, sauté onion 5 to 8 minutes until translucent. Add garlic and pepper; continue to cook for 3 to 5 minutes. Add rice to skillet and cook 3 to 4 minutes until rice turns slightly translucent. Add hot chicken stock; cook over high heat 3 to 5 minutes until rice starts to swell and absorb the liquid. Reduce heat and add lemon juice, chopped tomato, saffron and Tabasco. Cook uncovered 10 to 15 minutes, stirring occasionally, until liquid is absorbed and rice is tender. Stir in peas, parsley, salt and pepper. Put a mound of cooked rice on a serving platter or individual plate, top with grilled seafood and serve immediately.

Soak clams in enough lightly salted water to cover for 30 minutes. Drain and place on grill over high heat for 4 to 5 minutes until clams open. Discard any clams that do not open.

Brush shrimp and scallops with a little olive oil and sprinkle with a few drops of lemon juice. Cook sausage in a small covered skillet in $\frac{1}{3}$ cup white wine or water for 8 to 10 minutes until sausage is completely cooked and fat is rendered. Drain and cut into $\frac{3}{4}$-inch-thick slices. Alternate shrimps, scallops and sausage on presoaked wooden or metal skewers. Grill on high heat for 5 to 6 minutes until shrimp and scallops are firm to the touch.

FENNEL-FLAVORED RED SNAPPER

Servings: 2

A mini-chopper makes this a very quick marinade. Try this with halibut, swordfish or any other firm-fleshed fish. Serve with sliced tomatoes and fresh garden corn for a light summer dinner.

1 lb. red snapper fillets

MARINADE

5-6 peppercorns
1 tsp. fennel seed
1/8 tsp. red pepper flakes
1/2 tsp. salt

1 clove garlic, chopped
1 tbs. full-flavored olive oil
1 tbs. lemon juice

Combine peppercorns, fennel seed, red pepper flakes and salt in a mini-chopper or spice grinder. Process until very smooth. Add garlic, olive oil and lemon juice; process until creamy. With a sharp knife, lightly score fish on both sides. Spread marinade on both sides of fish and allow to stand 15 to 20 minutes before grilling. When the grill is hot, grill for 10 to 12 minutes or until fish is firm to the touch. Turn fish once during grilling. Serve immediately.

MUSTARD ROCK COD

Servings: 2

Rock cod, red snapper, halibut and other firm-fleshed fish are delicious when cooked on the grill. Use a few drops of Liquid Smoke to add a new dimension to the taste of foods cooked indoors.

10-12 oz. fillet of rock cod, about ¾-inch thick
1 tbs. olive oil
1 tbs. lemon juice
1 tbs. Dijon mustard
2 green onions, white part only, finely chopped
salt and white pepper
3-4 drops Liquid Smoke

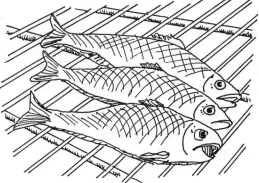

Combine olive oil, lemon juice, mustard, onions, seasonings, and Liquid Smoke and spread over fish. Allow to marinate 15 to 20 minutes before grilling. Grill on a preheated grill about 6 minutes each side, or until fish is firm to the touch. Serve immediately.

TUNA WITH
ZESTY TOMATO SAUCE

Keep the slices about ¾-inch thick so they grill evenly and don't overcook.

8 -10 oz. fresh tuna
olive oil

salt and pepper

Brush tuna with olive oil; season with salt and pepper. When grill is hot, cook tuna about 5 to 6 minutes each side, or until fish is slightly firm to the touch. Serve immediately with tomato sauce.

ZESTY TOMATO SAUCE

1 tbs. full-flavored olive oil
1 large clove garlic, minced
2 cups fresh tomato pieces (about 3
  large tomatoes, peeled, seeded,
  chopped)

2 tbs. finely chopped Italian parsley
dash red pepper flakes
salt and freshly ground pepper
5-6 black Kalamata olives, pitted,
  chopped

Heat olive oil in a medium skillet and cook garlic for a minute. Add tomatoes, parsley, red pepper flakes, salt and pepper; cook over medium high heat about 15 minutes until sauce has thickened. Stir in olives.

SWORDFISH WITH LEMON CAPER SAUCE

Servings: 2

Fresh swordfish is a real treat and grills well. Halibut or red snapper are also delicious with this sauce. Serve with a green salad and hot garlic bread.

10-12 oz. piece of swordfish, about 1 inch thick
olive oil
salt and pepper

LEMON CAPER SAUCE

2 tbs. olive oil
2 tbs. lemon juice
1 tbs. finely chopped parsley
2 tsp. capers, drained
salt and freshly ground pepper

Grill fish on a preheated grill about 8 minutes each side, or until fish is firm to the touch. Place on heated serving plates and spoon a little sauce over fish. Pass additional sauce. Serve immediately.

FISH TACOS

Use red snapper, rock cod, halibut or other firm-fleshed fish for this dish. Make the Spicy Corn Salsa first and heat preformed taco shells while the fish is grilling. This is a favorite summer dinner.

SPICY CORN SALSA

1 cup small frozen white corn, defrosted, or fresh corn kernels
1/3 cup diced red bell pepper
1 small jalapeño, seeded, finely minced, or to taste
1 large tomato, peeled, seeded, chopped
1 medium avocado, peeled, seeded diced
1 tbs. lime juice

1 tbs. light olive or vegetable oil
1 tsp. cumin
1/2 tsp. chile powder
1/2 tsp. dried oregano
2-3 green onions, finely chopped
salt and freshly ground black pepper
1/2 cup coarsely chopped fresh cilantro leaves

Combine ingredients tossing lightly with two forks. Set aside until fish is grilled.

8 oz. red snapper, halibut or other firm-fleshed fish
olive oil
salt and pepper
4-5 preformed small taco shells
1 cup shredded iceberg lettuce, optional

Cut fish into 1-inch cubes and thread on presoaked wooden skewers or metal skewers. Brush with olive oil and season with salt and pepper. Grill 3 to 4 minutes a side or until fish feels firm to the touch. Heat taco shells according to package directions while fish is grilling. To assemble: Place pieces of fish and some shredded lettuce in taco shell, top with salsa and enjoy!

LOBSTER TAILS
WITH GARLIC BUTTER

Grilled lobster makes a special dinner for two. The tails are generally frozen, so defrost them completely and grill for about 10 minutes per inch of thickness.

2 lobster tails, about 8 oz. each
2 tbs. butter
2 tbs. lemon juice
1 small clove garlic, finely chopped

With kitchen shears, remove flat underside of lobster shell. Loosen meat from shell, but keep it joined at the tail. Place lobster on the preheated grill shell side down; grill for about 12 minutes before turning over. Lobster is done when opaque and firm to the touch. In a small microwavable bowl, combine butter, lemon juice and garlic. Microwave to melt butter. Place lobster on serving plates and spoon some butter mixture over it. Serve immediately.

GRILLED POULTRY

Grilled chicken is almost a universal favorite. Not only is it widely available, but it cooks quickly, is delicious, and plays a significant role in healthful eating. If you don't have time for a lot of preparation, most supermarkets carry skinless boneless pieces, ready for the marinade. Turkey slices and ground poultry are also readily available, and great on the grill.

For more general hints on grilling, see page 5. Here are some safe and easy poultry grilling suggestions:

- Wash raw meat pieces carefully under cold water and dry before proceeding with the recipe.

- Refrigerate poultry while marinating. Remove from refrigerator a few minutes before grilling.

- Dark meat pieces take longer to cook than white meat. Grill meat to a temperature of at least 160°. The juices should run clear, not pink, and the meat should be firm to the touch.

- When arranging chunks of poultry on a skewer, leave about ¼-inch between pieces for more even cooking.

Chicken salads are always popular and we have included a *Far East Chicken Salad*, and a *Spicy Chicken and Pepper Salad*. Chicken breasts are grilled with honey teriyaki, wine, or curry marinades. If you like spicy food, try *Jamaican Jerk Rubbed Chicken*,

Peppered Chicken Breasts, or *Turkey with Charmoula Marinade*. Also on the spicy side are homemade *Turkey Chorizo Sausages* that are spectacular in many dishes, including pizza, eggs, or just grilled as the main event. *Indian-Style Chicken* makes an easy company meal with *Rice Pilaf* and a crisp green vegetable. Try *Turkey Tonnato* and *Chicken with Italian Salsa Verde* as part of a patio buffet or a picnic with some vegetable salads. Preheat the grill and prepare some of these super chicken and turkey taste treats.

HONEY TERIYAKI CHICKEN

Servings: 3-4

*This is a delicious marinade. Serve with **Rice Pilaf**, page 123, and a green vegetable.*

8 boneless, skinless chicken thighs
3 tbs. soy sauce
2 tbs. vegetable oil
1 tbs. honey
2 tbs. red wine vinegar

1 tbs. finely chopped onion
1 large clove garlic, minced
1 quarter-sized piece fresh ginger, minced
generous grind of fresh pepper

Cut each chicken thigh into 6 to 8 pieces, about 1 inch square. Combine remaining ingredients in a small bowl and marinate chicken pieces for at least 30 minutes before grilling, or several hours in the refrigerator. Remove from refrigerator about 30 minutes before grilling. Arrange chicken pieces on metal skewers or bamboo skewers that have been soaked in water for 15 to 20 minutes. Spray the grill with nonstick cooking spray and preheat grill with the rack as close to the heating element as possible. Cook chicken for about 8 to 10 minutes each side, or until chicken is firm to the touch and lightly browned. Serve immediately.

PEPPERED CHICKEN BREASTS

Servings: 2

This is a slightly spicy marinade. Start the chicken marinating when you get in the kitchen and by the time you put together a salad, cook a little rice or make some garlic bread, the chicken will be ready to grill.

2-3 skinless boneless chicken breasts
2 tbs. lemon juice
2 tbs. full-flavored olive oil
$\frac{1}{2}$ tsp. freshly ground black pepper
$\frac{1}{4}$ tsp. red pepper flakes
salt to taste

Combine ingredients and rub over chicken breasts. Allow to marinate about 30 minutes. Spray grill with nonstick cooking spray. Preheat grill to highest setting with rack as close as possible to cooking element. Cook chicken breasts about 4 minutes per side, depending on temperature of grill. Chicken is done when firm to the touch. Serve immediately.

CHICKEN WITH ITALIAN SALSA VERDE

Servings: 2

This sauce is great on hot pasta or fish, or put a little on your chicken sandwich.

4-5 skinless, boneless chicken thighs
1 tbs. olive oil
1 tsp. balsamic vinegar

1 small clove garlic, minced
salt and freshly ground pepper

SALSA VERDE

½ cup firmly packed Italian parsley
  leaves
2 tbs. drained capers
1 small shallot, about 1 tbs. chopped
1 large clove garlic

6 anchovy fillets, drained, patted dry
1 tsp. Dijon mustard
1 tbs. red wine vinegar
¼ cup full-flavored olive oil
freshly ground pepper

Cut each thigh into 6 equally-sized pieces and marinate for about 30 minutes in olive oil, vinegar, garlic, salt and pepper. Process salsa ingredients except olive oil in a food processor until mixture is in small pieces. Add olive oil and continue to process until well combined but still a little chunky. Allow to rest at room temperature for 30 minutes before serving, or refrigerate and return to room temperature before using. Thread chicken on presoaked wooden skewers or metal skewers and grill about 8 to 10 minutes each side, or until firm and lightly browned. Spoon salsa verde over meat and serve immediately.

MUSTARD GLAZED CHICKEN BREASTS

Servings: 2-3

Chicken breasts are marinated in a flavorful wine, mustard and honey mixture and then grilled. Serve with a fresh fruit salad, rice pilaf or couscous.

4 skinless, boneless chicken breasts

MARINADE

2 tbs. vegetable oil
1 tbs. honey
1 tbs. Dijon mustard

1 tbs. tomato paste
1/3 cup dry white wine
1 small garlic clove, minced
1 small shallot, finely chopped

Place chicken breasts in a plastic bag. Whisk marinade ingredients together and pour over chicken breasts. Marinate in the refrigerator for 3 to 4 hours or overnight turning 2 to 3 times. Remove from refrigerator 15 to 20 minutes before grilling. Cook chicken breasts 4 to 5 minutes each side, until chicken is firm to the touch and lightly browned. Serve immediately.

FAR EAST CHICKEN SALAD

Crisp hot pieces of grilled chicken thighs are tossed with lettuce, cilantro and a subtle peanut sesame seed dressing. Make the dressing before you start grilling the chicken so it has a chance to cool slightly. This works well in a double sided grill.

10-12 oz. boneless, skinless chicken thighs (about 4)

MARINADE

1 tbs. soy sauce
1 tbs. lemon juice
½ tsp. grated fresh ginger
1 tbs. vegetable oil

Combine marinade ingredients in a small bowl or plastic bag and marinate chicken in the refrigerator 2 hours, or longer. Remove from refrigerator 30 minutes before grilling. Discard marinade. Preheat the grill and cook chicken 7 to 8 minutes a side, until firm to the touch and no longer pink. Remove to a cutting board and cut into thin strips.

DRESSING

1 tbs. soy sauce
2 tbs. rice wine vinegar
1 tsp. sesame oil
$\frac{1}{2}$ tsp. grated fresh ginger
1 tbs. vegetable oil

1 tbs. water
2 tsp. sugar
$\frac{1}{2}$ tsp. dry hot mustard
1 tbs. peanut butter
1 clove garlic, minced

Bring dressing ingredients to a boil in a small saucepan and cook 2 to 3 minutes until sauce thickens slightly. Take saucepan off heat and allow to cool for a few minutes while chicken is grilling.

4-5 cups shredded iceberg lettuce
$\frac{1}{2}$ cup fresh cilantro leaves
2 green onions, slivered

1 tbs. toasted sesame seeds
$\frac{1}{2}$ cup packaged crisp chow mein
   noodles

Combine lettuce, cilantro, onions and sesame seeds in a shallow bowl or platter, toss with cooked dressing; top with grilled chicken pieces and chow mein noodles. Serve immediately. Boneless, skinless chicken breasts can be substituted for chicken thighs, just cook for a shorter time.

CHICKEN FAJITAS

Double this recipe and keep filling up the grill.

10-12 oz. boneless, skinless chicken thighs
4-5 flour tortillas
fresh cilantro leaves
sour cream
guacamole
salsa fresca
1 large red onion, peeled, sliced

MARINADE

2 tbs. lime juice
2 tbs. tequilla
1 tbs. vegetable oil
½ tsp. dried oregano
½ tsp. cumin
generous grinding of black pepper
olive oil

Flatten chicken pieces, or cut to make uniform in thickness. Place chicken in a bowl or plastic bag with marinade ingredients and marinate in the refrigerator for 2 to 3 hours. Remove from refrigerator about 30 minutes before grilling. Discard marinade. Grill chicken and onion slices over high heat 8 to 10 minutes each side until chicken is firm to the touch and no longer pink, and onions are nicely browned. Slice chicken into thin strips and serve in warm tortillas with onions, cilantro leaves, and sour cream, guacamole or salsa.

EASY GUACAMOLE

1 large ripe avocado
1 tsp. fresh lime juice
salt and freshly ground pepper
2 tbs. fresh salsa, or to taste
fresh cilantro leaves

Peel avocado, remove pit and coarsely mash fruit with a fork. Stir in remaining ingredients, season to taste and serve immediately with *Fresh Tomato Jalapeño Salsa*, page 128.

TURKEY WITH CRANBERRY ORANGE SAUCE

Thin turkey breast slices are grilled and served with a fruity cranberry orange sauce for a delicious low cal entrée. Serve with hot fluffy rice and fresh asparagus or broccoli.

2 oranges
1 cup cranberry juice cocktail
2 tsp. cornstarch dissolved in
  1 tbs. water
2-3 tbs. fresh or frozen
  cranberries, optional

salt and white pepper
1 lb. turkey breast slices
olive oil
salt and pepper

Grate rind from oranges. Remove peel and white membrane and cut out orange segments. Bring cranberry juice to a boil in a small saucepan. Add orange rind and dissolved cornstarch. Cook for 1 to 2 minutes until sauce thickens. Stir in orange slices, cranberries, salt and pepper. Keep warm over low heat.

Brush turkey slices with olive oil and season with salt and pepper. Grill 5 to 7 minutes a side, until turkey is firm to the touch. Do not overcook. Serve on heated plates and pour warm sauce over turkey slices.

TURKEY TONNATO

This is a great dish for a summer evening supper.

1 lb. turkey breast slices
olive oil

salt and lemon pepper

Brush turkey slices with olive oil and seasonings. Grill 5 to 7 minutes a side over high heat until firm to the touch. Remove from grill and cool while making dressing.

DRESSING

1 can (6½ oz.) tuna, drained
4 flat anchovies, rinsed, chopped
1 tsp. capers
1½ tsp. lemon juice
½ cup mayonnaise
dash Tabasco Sauce

generous amount of white pepper
¼ cup milk
roasted red pepper strips
black olives
parsley or watercress for garnish

Place tuna, anchovies, capers and lemon juice in food processor bowl; process 20 to 30 seconds. Add mayonnaise, Tabasco, white pepper and milk. Process until smooth. Refrigerate until ready to serve. Arrange turkey slices on a large plate and spoon dressing on each slice. Garnish with red pepper, olives and parsley. If turkey and sauce have been refrigerated for several hours, remove from refrigerator about 30 minutes before serving.

HAWAIIAN TURKEY KABOBS

*Tropical island flavors of rum, lime, ginger and honey make a delicious, quick, low fat marinade. Serve with **Mango Orange Salsa**, page 101, or **Creamy Peanut Sauce**, page 102.*

1-1½ lb. uncooked turkey breast	3 tbs. lime juice
3 tbs. honey	1 tbs. brown sugar
1 tbs. Dijon mustard	½ tsp. grated fresh ginger
3 tbs. dark rum	1 tsp. vegetable oil

Cut turkey breast into 1½-inch chunks and place in a glass or stainless steel bowl. Combine remaining ingredients and pour over turkey pieces. Marinate for about 30 minutes at room temperature. Thread turkey on metal or presoaked wooden skewers. Grill kabobs on a preheated grill for 10 to 12 minutes, basting with more sauce as they are turned. Serve immediately.

If there are leftovers, cut turkey into smaller pieces and combine with some of the salsa for a quick lunch box treat. Or tuck turkey pieces into a pita with some cucumber and tomato slices, and some cumin-flavored yogurt.

MANGO ORANGE SALSA

Makes: 2 cups

Here is a zesty, flavorful salsa that keeps for a couple of days in the refrigerator. It is great with grilled fish, meat or poultry.

1 ripe mango, peeled, cut into ¼-inch dice (about 1½ cups)
1 orange
1-2 jalapeño peppers, finely chopped, or to taste
2 tbs. red onion, finely chopped
¼ cup jicama, finely diced
1 tbs. chopped fresh mint
1 tsp. fresh lime juice
1 tsp. balsamic vinegar
freshly ground black pepper

Place diced mango into a glass or stainless steel bowl. Grate and add orange rind. Remove white membrane from orange sections by cutting off peel with a sharp knife. Cut orange segments away from membrane and chop orange pieces into ½-inch dice. Add remaining ingredients and mix well. Cover and refrigerate for about 30 minutes before serving.

CREAMY PEANUT SAUCE

Makes: ⅔ cup

This is a great dipping sauce for turkey, chicken or shrimp. Serve warm.

½ cup chicken stock
¼ cup smooth peanut butter
¼ tsp. finely chopped garlic
¼ tsp. finely grated fresh ginger
2 green onions, finely chopped
2 tsp. brown sugar
2 tsp. soy sauce
1 tsp. cider vinegar
dash red pepper flakes or ½ small fresh
 jalapeño pepper, minced
fresh cilantro leaves for garnish

Combine all ingredients in a small saucepan. Cook over low heat, stirring constantly, until mixture comes to a boil. Thin with a little stock if sauce seems too thick to spoon or dip. Keep warm until ready to serve, or make ahead and reheat.

DIJON TURKEY BURGERS

Servings: 4

Turkey burgers cooked on the grill make a great lunch or quick dinner. These are delicious served on onion or sesame rolls.

1 lb. ground turkey meat
1 tbs. Dijon mustard
½ tsp. vegetable oil
¼ tsp. dried tarragon or 2 tsp. finely
  chopped fresh
salt and freshly ground pepper

Combine seasonings with turkey meat and shape into 4 patties. Grill 4 to 6 minutes each side, or until internal temperature reaches 160°.

TURKEY CHORIZO SAUSAGES

Chorizo spices transform ground turkey into terrific, zesty sausages. Serve these in hot tortillas with shredded lettuce, lots of fresh cilantro leaves, a little guacamole or some sliced avocados, and a spoonful of fresh salsa. Or grill them for picnic fare and accompany with several salads, including a warm lentil or white bean salad. Leftovers can be sliced and used for a pizza topping or mixed with scrambled eggs for a hearty breakfast.

1 lb. ground turkey
2 tbs. chile powder
1/4 tsp. ground coriander
3 tbs. red wine vinegar
salt and freshly ground black pepper

Combine ingredients in a small bowl and refrigerate for 1 hour or longer. Divide mixture into 4 pieces and form into 5-inch long by 1 1/2-inch wide logs. Flatten to about 3/4-inch thickness. Cook on a preheated grill about 5 to 7 minutes per side.

LEMON CHICKEN

Grilled chicken breasts are topped with a piquant ginger lemon sauce. You can buy the sesame seeds pretoasted or toast them in a dry skillet over medium heat.

1 lb. boneless, skinless chicken breasts   olive oil, salt and pepper

Brush chicken breasts with olive oil and season with salt and pepper. Grill about 4 to 5 minutes a side, depending on thickness of chicken. Chicken should be firm to the touch and lightly browned.

½ cup chicken stock
rind and juice from 1 lemon (about
  ¼ cup)
2 tbs. brown sugar
1 tbs. soy sauce
¼ tsp. dry mustard

½ tsp. grated fresh ginger
1 tsp. cornstarch
1 tbs. water
1 tbs. toasted sesame seeds, optional
fresh watercress, cilantro or parsley for
  garnish

Bring chicken stock, lemon rind, juice, brown sugar, soy sauce, mustard and fresh ginger to a boil in a small saucepan. Dissolve cornstarch in 1 tbs. cold water and stir into sauce. Continue to cook over medium heat until sauce thickens. Pour over chicken, sprinkle on sesame seeds, garnish with watercress and serve.

SPICY CHICKEN AND PEPPER SALAD

Servings: 2

This zesty salad makes a great lunch or light dinner.

DRESSING

⅓ cup orange juice
1 tbs. full-flavored olive oil
1 tsp. apple cider vinegar
1 tsp. brown sugar
dash red pepper flakes
1 clove garlic, chopped
¼ tsp. cumin
salt and freshly ground pepper

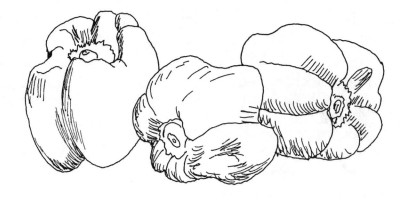

Combine dressing ingredients in a mini-chopper or blender and process until smooth. Pour into a small saucepan and bring to a boil. Remove from heat and allow to cool.

2 boneless, skinless chicken breasts
1 small red or yellow bell pepper, or half of each
1 tbs. olive oil
salt and freshly ground pepper
3-4 cups mixed salad greens
fresh cilantro for garnish

Flatten chicken breasts slightly. Remove seeds from pepper, and peel if desired. Cut into ½-inch strips. Toss pepper strips and chicken with olive oil. Season with salt and pepper. Grill chicken and pepper strips for 5 to 6 minutes each side, or until chicken is firm to the touch. Place salad greens on individual plates. Slice each breast into 6 or 7 thin slices. Arrange chicken and peppers over greens and spoon dressing on salad. Sprinkle with fresh cilantro leaves and serve immediately.

INDIAN-STYLE CHICKEN

A honey spice marinade gives these kabobs a rich brown color and wonderful flavor. Serve chicken on a bed of fresh cilantro leaves and accompany with a rice pilaf.

1 lb. boneless, skinless chicken thighs cut into 1-inch pieces
1 red or yellow bell pepper, seeded, cut into 1-inch squares
fresh cilantro for garnish

MARINADE

1 tbs. vegetable oil
1 tbs. lemon juice
3 tbs. honey
1 large clove garlic, minced
1 quarter-sized piece of fresh ginger,
  finely chopped

1 tsp. paprika
1 tsp. cumin
$\frac{1}{2}$ tsp. chili powder
salt and freshly ground pepper

Combine marinade ingredients in a mini-chopper or blender and process until smooth. Pour over chicken pieces and marinate for at least 30 minutes before cooking. Alternate chicken and red pepper pieces on presoaked wooden skewers or metal skewers. Grill about 8 to 10 minutes each side, or until chicken is firm and lightly browned; garnish with cilantro. Serve immediately.

GREEK-STYLE CHICKEN KABOBS

Servings: 2-3

*The simplest marinade of lemon juice, olive oil and oregano is particularly delicious on chicken. Serve this with the **Middle Eastern Cabbage Salad**, page 117, or use in place of the shrimp in the **Greek Shrimp Salad**, page 67.*

1 lb. boneless, skinless chicken thighs
  or chicken breasts
1 small red onion
lemon rind from 1 lemon
2 tbs. lemon juice

2 tbs. full-flavored olive oil
1 large clove garlic, minced
1/2 tsp. dried oregano
dash red pepper flakes
salt and freshly ground pepper

Cut chicken thighs into 1-inch pieces, or if using chicken breasts, cut each lengthwise into 2-inch-wide strips. Peel onion, cut into quarters and separate slices; cut slices into 1-inch pieces. Combine remaining ingredients and pour over chicken. Marinate at least 30 minutes before grilling. Drain marinade from chicken and set aside for later use. Alternate chicken thighs and onion pieces on presoaked wooden skewers or metal skewers. For chicken breasts, use 2 parallel skewers to keep pieces flat and place onions on a separate skewer. Grill thighs 8 to 10 minutes a side, breasts 2 to 3 minutes a side. Brush chicken with remaining marinade while grilling.

WINE MARINATED CHICKEN

Servings: 2-3

This is a quick and flavorful marinade for chicken breasts. Leftovers need only mayonnaise and arugula (a salad green with a peppery mustard flavor) to make a great sandwich.

1 lb. boneless, skinless chicken breasts, slightly flattened

MARINADE

2 tbs. olive oil
2 tbs. lemon juice
1/3 cup dry white wine
1 tsp. Dijon mustard

1 clove garlic, finely minced
1 tbs. finely chopped onion
1/2 tsp. dried thyme or 2-3 sprigs fresh
salt and freshly ground pepper

Combine marinade ingredients and pour over chicken breasts. Marinate in the refrigerator for an hour before grilling. Remove from marinade and cook on a preheated grill about 5 to 6 minutes each side, or until chicken is firm to the touch and lightly browned. Baste with marinade during grilling.

CURRIED CHICKEN BREASTS

Servings: 2-3

*Serve these lightly curried chicken breasts with **Rice Pilaf**, page 123, some chutney, and sliced pineapple or a fruit salad.*

1 lb. boneless, skinless chicken breasts, slightly flattened

MARINADE

2 tbs. butter
2 tbs. chopped onion
1 tsp. curry powder
1 clove garlic, minced
1 quarter-sized piece of fresh ginger,
 finely chopped

$\frac{1}{2}$ tsp. cumin
$\frac{1}{2}$ tsp. ground coriander
1 tbs. lemon juice
dash red pepper flakes
$\frac{1}{4}$ cup chicken stock
salt and freshly ground pepper

Melt butter in small skillet; saute onion 1 to 2 minutes until translucent. Add curry powder, garlic and ginger, and sauté another minute. Stir in remaining ingredients. Remove from heat, pour into a mini-chopper or blender and process until smooth. Pour mixture over chicken breasts and marinate in the refrigerator for about an hour before grilling. Grill on a preheated grill about 5 to 6 minutes a side, or until chicken is firm to the touch and lightly browned.

SESAME CHICKEN BREASTS

This full-flavored marinade uses the Korean flavors of sesame seeds, garlic and brown sugar.

1 lb. boneless, skinless chicken breasts, slightly flattened

MARINADE

2 tbs. soy sauce
2 tbs. dry sherry or Shao Shing
2 green onions, white part only, chopped
2 cloves garlic, chopped

2 tbs. brown sugar
1 tbs. toasted sesame seeds
½ tsp. sesame oil
dash red pepper flakes

GARNISH

1 tsp. toasted sesame seeds

fresh cilantro leaves

Combine marinade ingredients in a mini-chopper or blender and process until smooth. Pour over chicken breasts and marinate about 30 minutes before grilling. Grill chicken about 5 to 6 minutes each side, or until chicken is firm to the touch and lightly browned. Sprinkle with additional toasted sesame seeds and garnish with fresh cilantro leaves.

JAMAICAN JERK RUBBED CHICKEN

Servings: 2-3

If you like the spicy flavors of Caribbean food, you will love this marinade. Make a salad of avocado and orange slices drizzled with a little lime juice for a cooling accompaniment.

1 lb. boneless, skinless chicken breasts or thighs

MARINADE

½ cup chopped onion
juice of ½ lime
2-3 jalapeño peppers, seeds and ribs
  removed, coarsely chopped
½ tsp. thyme

½ tsp. allspice
¼ tsp. cinnamon
pinch of nutmeg
½ tsp. fresh ground black pepper
½ tsp. salt

Combine marinade ingredients in a blender and process to a smooth paste. Rub into chicken and marinate about 30 minutes at room temperature, or 2 to 3 hours in the refrigerator. Cook on preheated grill about 5 to 6 minutes a side, or until chicken is firm to the touch and lightly browned.

CORNISH GAME HEN

*With the size limitations of most indoor grills, it isn't feasible to do more than one Cornish game hen or small chicken at a time. A grilled fresh Cornish game hen will make a delicious dinner for two people. Serve with some **Grilled Polenta**, page 127, (it will fit around the sides of the hen), a crisp green vegetable and a fruity, red zinfandel or Beaujolais wine.*

1 Cornish game hen, about 20 oz.
5-6 lemon slices, thinly sliced
1 tbs. olive oil

1 tbs. lemon juice
dash red pepper flakes

Cut down both sides of backbone of game hen with a sharp knife or kitchen shears. Remove backbone so hen can be flattened. Wash and dry hen. Slip a lemon slice under skin of each thigh and remaining slices under skin covering breast. Combine olive oil, lemon juice and red pepper flakes. Place hen on a shallow plate and pour marinade over, coating both sides of hen. Marinate for about 30 minutes. Place on a preheated grill starting with skin side down. Cook for 20 to 25 minutes, turning several times, until internal temperature reaches 160° and hen is nicely browned.

SIDE DISHES AND ACCOMPANIMENTS

You can cook many things on a grill but sometimes an extra dish or two is needed to round out the menu. *Confetti Coleslaw* can be made ahead of time and keeps its crispness. *Middle Eastern Cabbage Salad* is great to tuck into pita breads with grilled meats, as are the two salsas. For a special dinner, make orange-flavored *Rice Pilaf* or *Rice Stuffed Tomatoes*.

Grilled Polenta is marvelous to have on hand in the refrigerator and keeps well for at least a week, if it lasts that long. This is a very easy basic baked polenta that can be made ahead and then sliced and grilled on demand.

Another excellent item to have in the refrigerator is roasted garlic. Bake several heads at a time and then use it for garlic bread, with a little butter for a vegetable sauce, or use it in *Bacon Wrapped Mushrooms*, page 31.

Another great side dish is couscous, the tiny Moroccan pasta. It cooks in 5 minutes and can be flavored with raisins, pine nuts and a little curry powder, or small pieces of cooked red peppers and onions, or chopped green chiles and cumin. It is also a delicious stuffing for tomatoes or peppers.

Here are some of our favorite side dishes for you to try.

MIDDLE EASTERN CABBAGE SALAD

This is an attractive crisp salad to accompany almost any grilled entrée.

2 cups thinly sliced cabbage
2 cups thinly sliced romaine or iceberg
  lettuce
3-4 minced green onions, white part
  only

1 orange
½ cup thinly sliced seeded cucumber
1 tbs. finely chopped fresh dill

Dressing

¼ cup olive oil
2 tbs. red wine vinegar
1 small clove garlic, minced
¼ tsp. dried oregano

¼ tsp. dried mint, or 3-4 fresh mint
  leaves, finely chopped
salt and freshly ground pepper

Combine cabbage, lettuce and onions in a medium bowl. With a sharp knife, cut off orange peel, removing white membrane at the same time. Separate orange into segments. Reserve in a small bowl. Squeeze any juice remaining in orange pulp into bowl to be used for dressing. Whisk dressing ingredients together to form an emulsion. Combine orange segments, cucumber slices and dill with salad greens, toss with salad dressing and serve immediately.

CONFETTI COLESLAW

Servings: 6

This crisp colorful salad has grated apples, carrots and red peppers mixed in with the cabbage. Whole grain mustard adds some zip to the dressing. This can be made ahead and keeps well for 2 to 3 days, refrigerated.

1 small head cabbage, about 1½ lbs.
2 medium apples, peeled, cored

2 medium carrots, peeled
1 medium red bell pepper

DRESSING

¾ cup mayonnaise
½ cup sour cream
¼ cup whole grain mustard, Creole-
style or Pommery

2 tbs. lemon juice
salt and generous amount of freshly
ground black pepper

Shred cabbage in food processor using the 1 milimeter slicing blade or slice thinly with a knife. Coarsely grate apples and carrots. Finely dice red pepper. Combine vegetables in a large bowl. Combine dressing ingredients and pour over vegetables. Mix well. Cover and refrigerate at least 2 hours or overnight before serving.

CREAMY POTATO SALAD

Servings: 6

Here is an old-fashioned potato salad with lots of pickle and onion. It is a great accompaniment to grilled meats and can be made a day ahead so the flavors have time to blend.

2 lb. boiling potatoes, peeled, cooked
3 eggs, hard-boiled
1/3 cup sweet pickles, finely chopped
1/3 cup sweet white or red onion, finely chopped
1/3 cup parsley, minced

1/2 cup mayonnaise
1/2 cup sour cream
2 tbs. Dijon mustard
salt and freshly ground pepper
paprika for garnish

Cut cooked potatoes into 3/4-inch cubes and coarsely chop eggs. Place in a large bowl with pickles, onion and parsley. Combine remaining ingredients except paprika in a small bowl and pour over potatoes. Mix gently until well combined (hands work well for this). Sprinkle top of salad with a little paprika. Cover and refrigerate until ready to serve.

PATIO PASTA SALAD

If you make this salad ahead, remove from refrigerator about 30 minutes before serving and add the fresh sweet basil.

8 oz. dried radiatore, gemellini, fusilli or pasta of your choice
1 tbs. full-flavored olive oil
$\frac{1}{3}$ cup finely chopped sweet red or white onion
1 small sweet red, green or yellow pepper, diced
1 medium celery stalk, thinly sliced
1 medium carrot, peeled, coarsely grated
1 medium tomato, peeled, seeded, chopped
dash red pepper flakes
1 tbs. Dijon mustard
3 tbs. full-flavored olive oil
1 tbs. rice wine vinegar
grated rind of 1 lemon
2 tsp. lemon juice
salt and freshly ground pepper
2 tbs. Italian parsley, finely chopped
$\frac{1}{3}$ cup grated Parmesan cheese
8-10 fresh sweet basil leaves cut into thin strips

Cook pasta according to package directions. Drain and rinse with cold water, drain again, and toss in a large bowl with 1 tbs. olive oil. Add chopped vegetables and pepper flakes. Whisk together mustard, olive oil, vinegar, lemon rind and juice, salt and pepper until mixture forms an emulsion. Toss pasta and vegetables with dressing and parsley. Stack basil leaves and cut into short thin strips. Top with Parmesan cheese and sweet basil. Serve immediately or refrigerate 1 to 2 hours or overnight.

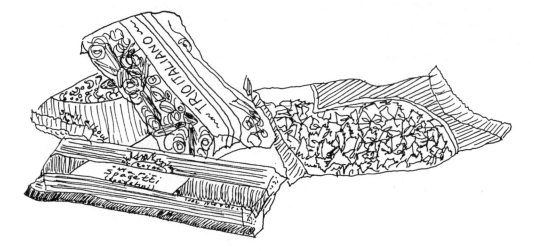

QUICK MEXICAN BEAN SALAD

Servings: 4-5

This hearty salad is delicious with grilled meats or chicken and can be done a day ahead.

1 can (15 oz.) red kidney beans or pinto beans
1 can (15 oz.) garbanzo beans
1 can (12 oz.) whole kernel corn
5-6 green onions, finely chopped
4-5 tbs. finely chopped canned green chiles
1 large tomato, peeled, seeded, chopped

1 tsp. ground cumin
1 tsp. dried oregano
1 tbs. lemon juice
2 tbs. finely chopped fresh cilantro
½ cup mayonnaise
salt and freshly ground black pepper
fresh cilantro leaves for garnish

Drain beans and corn, rinse well with cold water and drain again. Combine all ingredients except cilantro in a large bowl, gently tossing with 2 forks. Chill in refrigerator 2 hours before serving. Garnish with fresh cilantro leaves.

RICE PILAF

This orange-flavored pilaf is a great accompaniment for grilled chicken, pork or lamb. For a nice variation use dried cherries or currants and toasted pine nuts. Use one of the flavorful long grain rices such as Texmati, Jasmati or Mahatma.

3 tbs. butter
½ cup finely chopped onion
1 cup uncooked long grain rice
grated rind of 1 orange
juice of 2 oranges plus enough chicken broth to make 2 cups liquid
½ tsp. salt
slivered toasted almonds and white raisins

Melt butter in large saucepan. Sauté onion until soft but not brown. Add rice to pan and stir until rice is well coated with butter and starts to turn a milky or translucent color, about 5 minutes. Add orange rind, orange juice, chicken broth and salt. Bring to a boil. Cover and cook over low heat about 18 to 20 minutes, or until rice is tender and liquid is absorbed. Stir in slivered almonds and raisins.

RICE STUFFED TOMATOES

Servings: 4

If you are looking for something special to serve with grilled lamb or chicken, try these stuffed tomato cups. If you have some leftover cooked rice these go together quickly and can be heated in the oven just before serving.

4 large tomatoes
3 tbs. butter
3 tbs. minced shallots, or 6 green onions, white part only, thinly sliced
1 tsp. dried sweet basil
½ tsp. dried marjoram
½ tsp. salt
generous dash of white pepper
1½ cups cooked rice
grated Parmesan cheese
butter

Cut about ½-inch slice off top of tomatoes. Carefully cut around outside of tomato with a small knife, leaving a ½-inch shell. Remove tomato centers with a small sharp spoon and coarsely chop tomato flesh. Rinse out tomatoes to remove seeds and sprinkle inside of each tomato shell with a little salt. Turn shells upside down on a plate to drain for about 20 minutes. Heat butter in a small skillet. Sauté shallots or green onions 3 to 4 minutes until soft but not brown. Add basil, marjoram, salt, pepper, rice and chopped tomato centers to skillet. Mix well. Stuff tomato shells with rice mixture. Sprinkle with Parmesan cheese and dot with butter. Place tomatoes in a small baking dish with ½-inch of water in bottom of pan. Bake in a 375° oven about 15 minutes, or until tomatoes start to soften and are hot. Serve immediately.

VARIATION

Parboil red bell pepper shells for 5 minutes. Stuff with rice mixture, substituting ½ cup sliced sautéed fresh mushrooms for tomato pieces. Place in a baking pan with ½-inch water in bottom of pan. Bake uncovered for 20 minutes at 375°.

TEXAS TOAST WITH ROASTED GARLIC

Makes: 8 slices

This soft garlicky bread is terrific with grilled dishes. The garlic can be roasted ahead, and the soft pieces removed and refrigerated for 3 to 4 days. Or make the butter and refrigerate until ready to use. Roasted garlic is good in so many things—on hot vegetables, in mayonnaise, etc.—that you may want to roast several heads while you are doing it. Don't bother to peel off the outside papery skin before roasting.

1 whole head of garlic
olive oil

3 tbs. soft salted butter
dash white pepper

Cut about 1 inch off top of garlic head to expose tops of cloves. Drizzle with olive oil, wrap in foil and bake in a 350° oven for about 45 minutes or until cloves are soft. Unwrap and allow to cool. Dig out soft cooked cloves with tip of a small knife. If you squeeze from bottom, clove usually pops out easily. Combine cloves with butter and white pepper.

Purchase a deli specialty bread that is cut in 1-inch thick slices. If this is unavailable in your market, buy an unsliced sandwich loaf and cut it yourself. Toast bread slices on the grill until lightly browned on one side. Turn and spread toasted side generously with garlic butter, grill until second side is toasted. Serve hot.

GRILLED POLENTA

We have tried a lot of polenta cooking techniques but recently came across a simple one on the back of a polenta package that can be baked in the oven. Here is our adaptation.

2⅓ cups lukewarm water
½ tsp. salt
1 tbs. butter
¾ cup polenta (not instant)

pinch white pepper
3 tbs. grated Parmesan cheese
full-flavored olive oil or butter

Preheat oven to 350°. Pour water into an 8 x 8 inch baking pan and add salt and butter. Stir in polenta and white pepper. Place uncovered in oven and bake for 40 minutes. Stir polenta, add Parmesan cheese and continue to bake for an additional 10 to 15 minutes until polenta is firm and liquid has evaporated. Remove from oven and allow to cool.

Turn cooled polenta out of baking pan. Cut into 3-inch squares, brush with full-flavored olive oil or melted butter, and cook on preheated grill about 5 minutes each side, or until hot and lightly browned.

FRESH TOMATO JALAPEÑO SALSA

Makes: 1½ cups

Make this with ripe, full-flavored tomatoes and serve a spoonful with grilled turkey or chicken breasts in your fajitas or quesadillas, or add some to a ripe chopped avocado for a delicious guacamole.

¼ cup finely chopped red onion
4 medium-sized ripe tomatoes, finely chopped
1-2 jalapeño or serrano chilies, seeded, finely chopped, to taste
3 tbs. finely chopped fresh cilantro
2 tsp. fresh lime juice
½ tsp. salt
½ tsp. sugar

Combine all ingredients in a small ceramic or stainless steel bowl. Allow to marinate in the refrigerator about 30 minutes before serving.

PAPAYA AND AVOCADO SALSA

Makes: 2½ cups

This is a terrific salsa to complement any grilled meat, chicken or fish. Serve with chips for an appetizer, or spoon into a warm flour tortilla with some scrambled eggs.

1 large ripe papaya, peeled, seeded
1 large ripe avocado, peeled, seeded
grated rind from 1 lime
2 tbs. fresh lime juice
3 green onions, finely chopped
1-2 jalapeño peppers, seeded, finely minced
3 tbs. finely chopped fresh cilantro leaves
salt and freshly ground black pepper

Cut papaya and avocado into ½-inch pieces. Combine with remaining ingredients in a glass or stainless steel bowl, cover and refrigerate about 30 minutes before serving.

GRILLED VEGETABLES

Savory grilled vegetables are a nice change from the usual steamed or boiled versions. Lightly brushed with olive or vegetable oil, grilling brings out the toasty, caramel flavors of carrots and parsnips. Grilling is a superb technique for cooking eggplant because it takes only the lightest brushing of oil to coat the slices. In general, the natural flavors of grilled vegetables really come through and rich sauces or butter are superfluous.

If you need large quantities, several batches of vegetables can be grilled sequentially and then put together in a salad or reheated in the microwave. A real time saver for root or firm vegetables is to either blanch them in boiling water for several minutes or partially precook them in the microwave before grilling. We use the microwave for precooking new potatoes, carrots, fennel, and eggplant. The partially cooked vegetables can then be finished on the grill in a matter of minutes. Root vegetables will grill nicely without precooking and the texture will be a little firmer than those microwaved or blanched.

See grilling tips, page 5.

Grilled Carrots and *Toasty Yukon Gold* or new potatoes are great examples of how wonderful grilled vegetables can be. Try some of the eggplant recipes, too. *Pepper Boats* are delicious as part of an antipasto platter or as a vegetable side dish. *Stuffed Tomatoes with Goat Cheese* are good first course or cheese course fare for entertaining.

Grilled apples are marvelous especially when paired with sweet potatoes and celery root. Both of these recipes are well suited for holiday dinners. Pearl onions are toasty and sweet, without the cook having to do the tedious peeling. Grilling is our current favorite preparation for okra; when grilled it gets crisp and full-flavored—great finger food.

Buy the freshest high quality produce you can find and try grilling vegetables!

GRILLED CARROTS

Grilled carrots are wonderful. They turn golden brown as the natural sugars are caramelized. You could also just brush them with a full-flavored olive oil if you didn't want to make the garlic olive oil marinade.

4 large garlic cloves, peeled, smashed
2 tbs. full-flavored olive oil
dash red pepper flakes
2-3 large carrots, peeled, sliced into ¼-inch thick by 2-3 inch long pieces

Place garlic cloves, olive oil and red pepper flakes in a small heavy saucepan or skillet. Sauté over medium heat until garlic has browned. Remove from heat and allow to cool. Discard browned garlic cloves. Place sliced carrots in a microwavable dish with 2 tbs. water. Cover and microwave on high for 2 minutes. Remove from microwave and dry carrots on paper towels. Toss carrots in garlic olive oil. Preheat the grill. When hot, cook carrots for about 4 minutes each side, depending on temperature of grill, until lightly browned and tender when tested with a fork. Cooked carrots may be placed in a warm oven for a few minutes until ready to serve.
NOTE: Small whole peeled carrots can be grilled as well. Precook for 3 to 4 minutes in the microwave before grilling.

NEW POTATO SALAD

Small new potatoes, red peppers and red onions are grilled and make a terrific accompaniment for roasted or grilled meats, or as part of a salad selection. This salad can be made well ahead and refrigerated. Bring to room temperature before serving.

1 medium red onion, peeled, cut into ½-inch slices
1 large red bell pepper
1 lb. small new potatoes, 1-to 1½-inch diameter
olive oil

DRESSING

4 tbs. olive oil
2 tsp. rice wine vinegar
1 tsp. lemon juice
¼ tsp. cumin
salt and freshly ground pepper

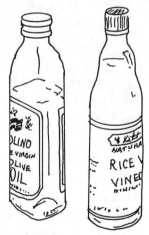

Preheat the grill. Place a skewer horizontally through onion slices to hold them together so they won't fall through rack unless using a rack with small openings. Brush onion slices with olive oil and place on grill with whole red pepper. Turn pepper frequently so all sides char. Turn onion slices 2 to 3 times and grill for about 10 minutes until softened. When pepper is roasted, remove and place on a plate, cover with a bowl to steam for about 15 minutes and then remove skin. Discard seeds and cut into ¾-inch squares. Precook unpeeled potates in microwave or boil until tender but firm, about 25 minutes. Pat dry and brush with olive oil. Grill for about 6 to 8 minutes until skins are lightly browned.

Combine dressing ingredients. When vegetables are cool enough to handle, slice potatoes into 3 to 4 slices each, and cut grilled onions into large dice. Combine potatoes, peppers and onions in a serving bowl and pour dressing over them. Gently spoon dressing from bottom of dish and distribute over vegetables once or twice instead of tossing vegetables. Serve warm or at room temperature.

SWEET CORN

Cooking sweet corn on the grill involves wrapping the ears of corn in foil or pulling back the husks, removing the silk, tying up the husks and soaking in cold water for a few minutes before grilling. We like to boil or steam the corn in advance; brush with flavored butter and grill for 3 to 4 minutes to heat through just before serving. Here are three great flavored butters for corn. Each is enough for 3 to 4 ears of corn.

BUTTER AND GARLIC TOPPING

2 tbs. butter
2 tbs. light olive oil
1 large clove garlic, finely minced

Combine butter, olive oil and garlic in a small microwavable bowl. Microwave for 30 to 45 seconds on high, until butter has melted. Brush on cooked corn and grill for 3 to 4 minutes or until corn is hot. Serve immediately.

SPICY CHILE BUTTER

2 tbs. butter
½ tsp. cumin
¼ tsp. dried oregano
¼ tsp. chile powder
1 tsp. lemon or lime juice

Melt butter; combine with seasonings and brush on cooked corn. Grill 3 to 4 minutes, turning frequently. Serve immediately.

BUTTER AND PARMESAN CHEESE

2 tbs. butter, melted
1 tbs. grated Parmesan cheese

Combine butter with Parmesan cheese; brush on cooked corn. Grill 3 to 4 minutes, turning frequently. Serve immediately.

TOASTY YUKON GOLD POTATOES

Servings: 3-4

Yellow-fleshed Yukon Gold potatoes are marvelous grilled and become very creamy and sweet. Cook as many as your grill will hold and they will disappear. You can precook the potatoes and grill at the last minute.

12-16 small new Yukon Gold or red potatoes
1 tbs. full-flavored olive oil
salt and pepper

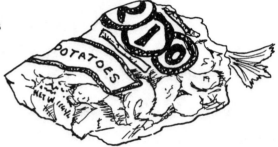

Start potatoes in cold water, cover and cook for about 30 minutes, or until barely tender. Drain and allow to stand until you are ready to grill. Pour olive oil onto a flat plate; season with salt and pepper and roll cooked potatoes until all sides are coated. Arrange potatoes on a preheated grill and cook 10 to 15 minutes, turning once or twice until all sides are nicely browned. Serve immediately.

PEPPER BOATS

Make this when summer tomatoes are plentiful and full of flavor. Serve hot or at room temperature.

2 large or 4 small red or yellow bell
  peppers
1 tbs. full-flavored olive oil
3 cups peeled, seeded, coarsely
  chopped tomatoes
2 garlic cloves, minced
5-6 green onions, finely chopped
1/2 tsp. dried oregano

3 tbs. finely chopped fresh sweet basil
1 sprig fresh thyme or 1/4 tsp. dried
salt and freshly ground pepper
grated Parmesan cheese or thin slices
  of fontina cheese
small black olives for garnish

Cut each large pepper into 4 sections to make small boats, or halve smaller peppers. Parboil peppers 3 to 4 minutes or microwave until peppers are slightly softened but still keep their shape. Heat olive oil in a medium skillet. Add tomatoes, garlic, onions, herbs, salt and pepper. Cook over medium high heat 6 to 8 minutes until tomato juices have been absorbed and mixture is slightly thickened. Spoon tomato sauce into precooked pepper halves. Top each pepper with 1 to 2 tsp. grated Parmesan cheese or a thin slice of fontina. When ready to serve, heat 3 to 4 minutes on a hot grill. Garnish with small black olives.

SUMMER VEGETABLE SALAD

Any combination of fresh vegetables can be grilled and served as a salad. Do the grilling ahead of time and allow the flavors to combine. Potatoes and carrots need to be parboiled or microwaved for 2 minutes before cooking on the grill.

1 small red bell pepper
4 large cloves garlic, peeled
2 large carrots, peeled, cut into $\frac{1}{4}$-inch by 3-4 inch slices
1-2 small zucchini, cut into $\frac{1}{4}$-inch by 3-4 inch slices
1-2 yellow squash, cut into $\frac{1}{4}$-inch by 3-4 inch slices
1 small red onion, cut into $\frac{1}{2}$-inch slices
6-8 medium mushrooms, cut in half
olive oil for grilling
1 medium tomato, peeled, seeded, chopped
1 tbs. full-flavored olive oil
1 tsp. balsamic or rice wine vinegar
$\frac{1}{2}$ tsp. fresh thyme or oregano leaves
salt and freshly ground pepper

Preheat the grill. Roast pepper on grill, turning to char all sides. Brush with olive oil and start roasting garlic because it will take 15 to 20 minutes. Place carrots in a microwavable dish with 2 tbs. water and cover. Microwave on high for 2 minutes. Remove, drain and pat dry. Brush carrots, zucchini, squash, onion and mushrooms with olive oil. Grill vegetables in turn until lightly browned and tender. Place in a shallow serving bowl or on a plate. Add chopped tomato and squeeze soft grilled garlic over vegetables. Combine olive oil, vinegar, thyme, salt and pepper. Pour over vegetables and toss lightly to combine. Serve at room temperature, or refrigerate and bring to room temperature before serving.

EGGPLANT WITH
YOGURT GARLIC SAUCE

Servings: 2-3

Soften the eggplant in the microwave; then grill to bring out its flavor. Serve at room temperature.

3-4 small Japanese or Chinese eggplants, or 1 small regular eggplant, about 1 lb.
1 red or green bell pepper
olive oil
½ cup yogurt
1 clove garlic, finely chopped with ¼ tsp. salt
1 small jalapeño pepper, seeded, minced
½ tsp. cumin
1 sprig fresh thyme leaves
salt and freshly ground pepper to taste
fresh cilantro leaves for garnish

142 VEGETABLES

Cut eggplant into thin slices, about ¼-inch thick. Microwave 2 to 3 slices at a time for 2 minutes on high, uncovered. Remove, place on paper towel to drain, and microwave remaining eggplant slices. Preheat grill; roast red pepper until skin is blistered on all sides, turning frequently. Remove from grill; place under a bowl to steam for 10 to 15 minutes before peeling. Remove skin and seeds. Slice into thin strips and place on a serving platter. Brush eggplant slices with olive oil and grill 10 to 12 minutes until soft and lightly browned. Place eggplant on peppers. Combine yogurt, garlic, jalapeño pepper, cumin, thyme, salt and pepper. Spoon over eggplant and peppers. Garnish with cilantro leaves.

EGGPLANT AND PEPPERS

Servings: 2-3

This is a great dish to keep in the refrigerator to serve as a quick vegetable side dish, or use as a topping for bruschetta for a quick appetizer. This works best on a screen or grill rack with small mesh to keep the vegetables from falling through.

2 red bell peppers
3-4 thin Chinese or Japanese eggplant
olive oil for grilling
1/4 cup full-flavored olive oil
2 tbs. balsamic or rice wine vinegar

1 large garlic clove, minced
1 tsp. minced fresh oregano or
 1/2 tsp. dried
salt and freshly ground pepper

Roast peppers on a preheated grill, turning frequently so all sides char. Place peppers under a small bowl or in a plastic bag to steam for about 15 minutes. Skin should pull off easily after steaming. Discard stem and seeds. Cut into about strips 1/4-inch wide.

Remove eggplant stems and cut in half horizontally. Cut into slices about 1/4-inch thick by 2 to 3 inches long. Place 5 to 6 eggplant slices on a microwavable plate and microwave for 2 minutes uncovered. Remove and drain slices on paper towels. Repeat with remaining eggplant slices. Lightly brush cooked eggplant slices with olive oil and grill about 2 minutes each side until lightly browned.

Combine oil, vinegar, garlic, oregano, salt and pepper on a large plate. Remove grilled eggplant slices and immediately put them in oil mixture on plate, turning to coat both sides. Continue process until all eggplant is cooked and coated. Add cooked red pepper strips to the plate. Serve at room temperature, or refrigerate for 4 to 5 days and use as desired.

SERVING SUGGESTIONS

Bruschetta: Toast $^3/_4$-inch thick slices of Italian, French or sourdough bread on one side. On toasted side, place 2 to 3 slices of drained eggplant and peppers, and put back on grill to toast bottom side of bread. Or top eggplant and peppers with Parmesan cheese and place under the broiler. Cut each slice into 3 to 4 pieces and serve immediately.

Pizza topping: Roll out crust and spread a layer of mozzarella cheese over it. Arrange eggplant and pepper slices over cheese, top with Parmesan cheese and bake until crust is done. Sprinkle baked pizza with pieces of peeled, seeded and chopped fresh tomato just before serving.

Pasta: Cut eggplant and peppers into 1-inch pieces and toss with hot cooked pasta. Use some of the flavorful marinating garlic oil, too. Sprinkle with Parmesan cheese.

EGGPLANT SANDWICHES

Grilled eggplant slices with a savory stuffing are reheated on the grill for a delicious snack or side dish. After precooking the eggplant in the microwave, it only takes a light brushing of olive oil before grilling. These are also good at room temperature.

12 slices eggplant, 3-inch diameter by $\frac{1}{2}$-inch thick
1 tbs. full-flavored olive oil

Place 3 eggplant slices on a microwavable plate and cook uncovered on high for 3 minutes. Remove from microwave and drain on paper towels. Repeat process until all slices have been cooked. Pat slices dry and brush both sides with olive oil. Place slices on a preheated grill and cook for 2 to 3 minutes per side until slices are lightly browned. Remove from grill and allow to cool. Spread with one of the following fillings and reheat on grill, turning over once just to warm eggplant and filling.

GREEK OLIVE AND GOAT CHEESE FILLING

2 tsp. full-flavored olive oil
1 small clove garlic, minced
2 oz. mild goat cheese or feta cheese
1 tbs. grated Parmesan cheese
½ tsp. fresh thyme leaves
6-8 small fresh basil leaves, cut into thin ribbons
4-5 Kalamata olives, pitted, finely chopped
salt and freshly ground black pepper

Heat olive oil in a small skillet and sauté garlic until soft but not browned. Let cool slightly before adding to cheese mixture. In a small bowl, combine goat cheese and Parmesan cheese. Mash cheeses with a fork; then add remaining ingredients, mixing well. Spread 2 to 3 teaspoons of filling on 6 grilled eggplant slices and top with remaining eggplant slices to make a sandwich. Reheat on grill before serving.

SUN-DRIED TOMATO FILLING

2 oz. mild goat cheese or cream cheese
1 tbs. grated Parmesan cheese
1 tbs. chopped sun-dried tomatoes in oil or rehydrated
2 tsp. full-flavored olive oil, or use some of the tomato oil
10-12 small fresh sweet basil leaves, cut into ribbons
dash hot pepper flakes
salt and freshly ground pepper

Mash cheese in a small bowl with a fork. Add remaining ingredients, mixing well. Mixture should be moist and spreadable. Spread 2 to 3 teaspoons of filling on 6 grilled eggplant slices and top with remaining eggplant slices to make a sandwich. Reheat on grill before serving.

FONTINA CHEESE AND PROSCIUTTO FILLING

6 thin slices fontina cheese, cut the same size as the eggplant

$\frac{1}{3}$ cup thinly sliced, coarsely chopped prosciutto, most of fat removed
2 tsp. Dijon mustard
1 tbs. chopped fresh sweet basil leaves
salt and freshly ground pepper

Combine prosciutto with remaining ingredients. Spread a small amount of filling on 1 side of each grilled eggplant slice. Top 6 slices of eggplant with fontina cheese and place remaining eggplant slices, topping side down, over cheese. Grill sandwiches 1 to 2 minutes per side until cheese melts.

CELERY ROOT
AND APPLE SLICES

Celery root and apples make a delicious combination and a terrific accompaniment for grilled chicken, pork or sausages. Smaller celery roots have better texture and solid centers.

1 small celery root	1 tsp. lemon juice
olive oil	1 tsp. butter
2 medium Golden Delicious apples	2 tbs. apple juice
vegetable oil	salt and freshly ground pepper

Cut top and bottom off celery root. Peel it, cutting into white flesh about $1/16$ -inch. Cut into thin slices about $1/8$-inch thick. Brush with olive oil and cook on a preheated grill on medium heat about 5 to 6 minutes a side, or until lightly browned and tender when pierced with tip of a knife. Core apples and cut horizontally into $1/4$-inch round slices. Brush with vegetable oil and grill 4 to 5 minutes a side, turning once or twice, until soft but firm. Alternate slices of grilled celery root and apples on a small platter. Combine lemon juice, butter, apple juice and salt and pepper in a small saucepan. Bring sauce to a boil and drizzle over apples and celery root.

SWEET POTATO
AND APPLE SLICES

This is a delicious side dish for a holiday dinner or for grilled pork chops.

2 small sweet potatoes or yams
2 medium golden delicious apples
vegetable oil
2 tbs. apple juice
2 tbs. maple syrup

$\frac{1}{4}$ tsp. cinnamon
generous dash nutmeg
1 tbs. butter
salt and freshly ground pepper

Peel sweet potatoes and cut into $\frac{1}{4}$-inch thick slices. Brush with oil and cook on a preheated grill 5 to 6 minutes a side, until lightly browned and tender when tested with a fork. Core apples and cut horizontally into $\frac{1}{4}$-inch round slices. Brush with oil and grill 4 to 5 minutes a side, turning once or twice, until soft but firm. Alternate slices of grilled sweet potato and apples on a serving plate. Combine apple juice, maple syrup, spices, butter, salt and pepper in a small saucepan. Bring sauce to a boil and drizzle over sweet potatoes and apples.

PEARL ONIONS

Here is an easy way to get around the tedious job of peeling small white boiling onions. The outside papery skin chars a little during the grilling and easily slips off, leaving the tender onion ready to eat. You can do several skewers of these ahead of time and serve at room temperature or reheat in the microwave.

10-12 oz. (about 20) small white boiling   salt
  onions, 1-1¼-inch diameter   1 tsp. white wine or balsamic vinegar
vegetable or olive oil

Cut off both ends of onions. Place a little vegetable or olive oil on a plate and roll onions to coat all sides. Arrange onions on presoaked wooden skewers or metal skewers, with the skewer going through the cut ends. Cook on a preheated grill 20 to 25 minutes, turning frequently, until onions are nicely browned and tender when pierced with a knife. Remove to a serving bowl, slip off papery skin and sprinkle with a little salt and white wine vinegar.

VARIATION

Grilled Shallots: Choose shallots of the same size, and grill the same way described in **Pearl Onions**. Sprinkle with salt and pepper. Balsamic vinegar marries perfectly with sweet grilled shallots.

OKRA WITH PESTO SAUCE

Servings: 2-3

Grilling transforms okra into a new tasting vegetable that even non-okra lovers enjoy or at least tolerate. The okra gets brown and slightly crisp. This is a great finger food appetizer. Use of the smaller mesh grill racks keeps the okra in line.

8-10 oz. fresh okra
full-flavored olive oil
salt

Trim stem end of okra. Pour olive oil onto a small plate, add a little salt and roll okra in oil to coat. Cook on a preheated grill about 12 to 15 minutes, turning frequently. Remove to a serving dish. Spoon some sauce over okra or serve sauce as a dip.

SAUCE

½ cup light sour cream or yogurt
2 tbs. prepared pesto sauce
½ tsp. lemon juice
salt and freshly ground pepper

Combine sour cream, pesto sauce, lemon juice, salt and pepper. Mix well and serve.

STUFFED TOMATOES WITH GOAT CHEESE

This makes a stunning first course or after the main course salad.

2 Roma or plum tomatoes
salt
1 tbs. full-flavored olive oil
1 large clove garlic, minced
dash red pepper flakes
¼ tsp. dried thyme or 1 tsp. fresh
salt and freshly ground pepper
4 tbs. fresh creamy goat cheese
¼ cup toasted pine nuts
4-5 cups fresh mixed lettuce pieces

DRESSING

1 tsp. red or white wine vinegar
1 tbs. full-flavored olive oil
salt and freshly ground pepper

Cut tomatoes in half lengthwise to make oval cups. Trim stem end and scoop out pulp and seeds. Sprinkle with salt and turn upside down on paper towels to drain for 15 to 20 minutes. In a small skillet, heat olive oil and sauté garlic with red pepper flakes for 1 to 2 minutes just to soften. Add thyme and a little salt and pepper. Remove from heat and allow to cool. Divide goat cheese among tomato cups. Drizzle olive oil/ garlic mixture over each cup and sprinkle with pine nuts. When ready to serve, grill tomatoes about 4 to 5 minutes until cheese is warmed. While tomatoes are grilling, combine vinegar, olive oil, salt and pepper and toss with lettuce pieces. Arrange greens on 4 individual salad plates leaving a small space in center. Place warm tomato boat in center of salad greens. Serve immediately.

PARSNIPS

If you think you don't like parsnips, try grilling them. They have a lemony toasty finish and just need a little salt, pepper and lemon juice to bring out their best flavors. The larger ones are the best ones to grill.

¾ lb. parsnips (4 medium)
olive oil
lemon juice
salt and pepper

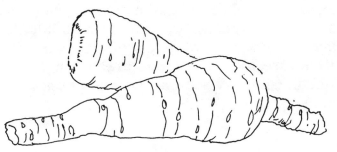

Cut off tops and bottoms of parsnips. No need to peel. Cut into ¼-inch thick slices, lengthwise. Brush with olive oil and grill about 8 to 10 minutes or until parsnips are tender and lightly browned. Sprinkle with a little lemon juice, salt and pepper. Serve warm.

RADICCHIO

Choose the smaller heads of radicchio for grilling. Radicchio looks great on the plate and has a sharp and slightly bitter flavor.

2 small heads of radicchio
olive oil
8 thin slices fontina cheese,
  approximately 1 inch by 3 inches
grated Parmesan cheese
salt and pepper

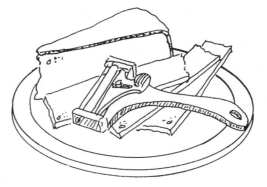

Cut each head of radicchio into quarters. Generously brush with olive oil and grill abut 8 to 10 minutes, turning to cook all sides. Radicchio is done when core is easily pierced with a knive. Sprinkle with salt and pepper. Top with cheese for last minute on the grill, or sprinkle with Parmesan after removing from the grill. Drizzle with a few drops of olive oil while still hot.

ZUCCHINI SLICES

Thin zucchini slices grill to a toasty brown in just a few minutes on the grill.

2 to 3 medium zucchini
full-flavored olive oil
salt and pepper

Cut off tops and ends of zucchini. Cut into ⅛- to ¼-inch slices. Brush with olive oil; sprinkle with salt and pepper. Cook on a preheated grill about 5 to 6 minutes, turning frequently. Cook to crisp-tender or soft, as you prefer.

GRILLED SANDWICHES

Warm toasted sandwiches are a breeze to make on any of the indoor grills. It is important to brush the outside pieces of bread with a little olive oil or melted butter to help the browning process.

Deli meats are great for quick sandwiches, but think about hot grilled sandwiches using skinless, boneless chicken breasts, hot dogs or precooked sausages. Toast the bread at the same time the meat is grilling, slather the hot bread with mayonnaise or mustard, and tuck in lettuce, tomato, sauerkraut, or avocado to complement your masterpiece. *South American Salsa,* is a great addition to sandwiches.

Placing a slice of cheese between two slices of deli meat, then grilling until the cheese starts to melt ensures that the filling will be warmed through.

Another favorite technique is to slip a slice of ripe tomato, crispy lettuce or thinly sliced pickles into the center of the grilled sandwich just before eating to provide texture and flavor contrast. If using one of the hinged grills, grill 2 to 3 thin slices of onion or pineapple and add them to your warm sandwich.

Wrapping prepared sandwiches in foil and heating them on the grill is a good way to make sandwiches for a group. All the work can be done ahead of time.

Here are some ideas for grilled sandwich combinations, but put together your favorites and have a good lunch!

ROAST BEEF ON RYE

Makes: 2 sandwiches

4 slices light or dark rye bread
olive oil
2 tbs. softened blue cheese
1 tsp. softened butter

½ tsp. Worcestershire sauce
¼ tsp. prepared horseradish
4 slices thin sliced roast beef

Brush outside of bread with olive oil. Mix cheese, butter, Worcestershire and horseradish together until creamy. Spread inside bread. Top with roast beef. Place slices together and grill 3 to 4 minutes, turning once, until outside bread is lightly browned and slightly crisp.

TURKEY ON WHOLE WHEAT

Makes: 2 sandwiches

4 slices whole wheat bread
olive oil
Dijon or other favorite mustard
4-5 thin slices turkey

2-3 slices provolone or smoked Gouda
  cheese
3-4 thin strips pimiento or oil packed
  sun-dried tomatoes

Brush outside of bread with olive oil. Spread inside with mustard and top with half the turkey, cheese, pimiento, remaining turkey and top slice of bread. Grill 3 to 4 minutes, turning once, until outside of bread is lightly browned and slightly crisp.

PASTRAMI AND SWISS

4 slices dark or light rye bread
olive oil
mustard
4-5 thin slices pastrami or corned beef
2-3 thin slices Swiss cheese
dill pickles, optional

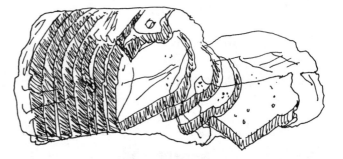

Brush outside of bread with olive oil. Spread inside of bread with mustard and top with half the pastrami, cheese, remaining pastrami and top slice of bread. Grill 3 to 4 minutes, turning once, until outside of bread is lightly browned and slightly crisp. Tuck in some sliced dill pickles or serve on the side.

HAM AND HOT PEPPER CHEESE

Makes: 2 sandwiches

4 slices dark or light rye bread
olive oil
Dijon mustard
4-5 thin slices of Virginia or Black Forest ham
2-3 slices hot pepper cheese
fresh tomato slices, optional

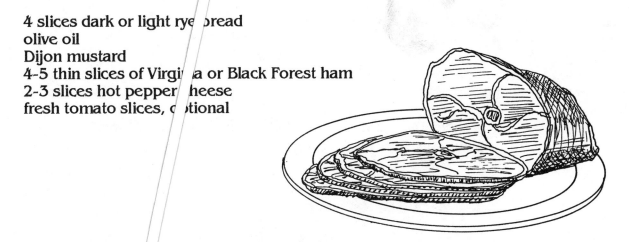

Brush outside of bread with olive oil. Spread mustard on inside. Top with half the ham, cheese, remaining ham and top slice of bread. Grill until bread is lightly browned and slightly crisp. Add fresh tomato slices to sandwich and serve.

TUNA

4 slices whole wheat or sourdough bread
olive oil
1 can (6½ oz.) water packed tuna, drained
2-3 tbs. mayonnaise, just to moisten
1 tsp. mustard
⅓ cup diced cheddar cheese
2-3 green onions, finely chopped

Brush outside of bread with a little olive oil. Combine remaining ingredients and spread on bread. Grill until bread is lightly browned and slightly crisp.

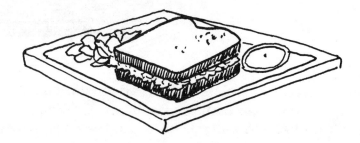

CHICKEN

2 Dutch Crunch or other sandwich rolls
olive oil
2 boneless, skinless chicken breasts, slightly flattened
Dijon, honey or sweet Russian mustard
salt and pepper
grilled onions, crisp green watercress or arugula

Split sandwich rolls, brush with olive oil and toast on grill at same time as chicken. Spread mustard on both sides of chicken; sprinkle with salt and pepper. Grill 5 to 6 minutes each side, until chicken is firm to the touch. If you are doing onions, brush onion slices with olive oil and grill at same time as chicken. Put a toothpick through onion slices to hold them together. Assemble sandwiches and serve immediately.

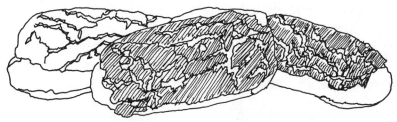

VEGETABLE

2 pita breads
fresh goat or cream cheese
1 large red bell pepper
2 small Japanese eggplants, cut into ⅛-inch slices
6 green onions
olive oil
salt and freshly ground pepper
fresh sweet basil leaves
capers

Cut pita breads in half; spread a little goat cheese inside. Cut peppers and eggplant into thin slices. Cut green tops off onions and coat with olive oil. Cook on a preheated grill for 5 to 6 minutes until vegetables are soft and lightly browned. Season generously with salt and pepper. Fill pita breads with grilled vegetables, adding some fresh basil leaves and a few capers. Warm sandwiches on grill just before serving.

INDEX

Spareribs, plum glazed
49
Spicy chicken and
pepper salad 106
Spicy chile butter 137
Spicy corn salsa 84
Steak
flank 44
island marinated 42
Stuffed tomatoes with
goat cheese 154
Summer vegetable
salad 140
Sun-dried tomato
filling 148
Super burgers 41
Sweet corn 136
Sweet potato and
apple slices 151
Swiss chard bundles 30
Swordfish with lemon
caper sauce 83

Tacos, fish 84
Teriyaki beef and
vegetable rolls 13

Texas toast with
roasted garlic 126
Thai beef satay 36
Thai-style dipping
sauce 23
Thyme lamb chops 54
Toasty Yukon gold
potatoes 138
Tools 3
Trout amandine 70
Tuna sandwich 164
Tuna with zesty
tomato sauce 82
Turkey
chorizo sausages 104
Dijon roll-ups 22
on whole wheat
sandwich 161
tonnato 99
with cranberry
orange sauce 98
Turkish-style lamb 55

Vegetable sandwich 166

Walnut, scallop and
avocado salad 64

Wine marinated
chicken 110

Yogurt cucumber
sauce 39
Yogurt marinated pork
chops 51

Zesty tomato sauce for
tuna 81
Zucchini slices 158

SERVE CREATIVE, EASY, NUTRITIOUS MEALS WITH NITTY GRITTY® COOKBOOKS

Cappuccino/Espresso: The Book of Beverages
Worldwide Sourdoughs From Your Bread Machine
Indoor Grilling
Slow Cooking
The Best Pizza is Made at Home
The Well Dressed Potato
Convection Oven Cookery
The Steamer Cookbook
The Pasta Machine Cookbook
The Versatile Rice Cooker
The Dehydrator Cookbook
The Bread Machine Cookbook
The Bread Machine Cookbook II
The Bread Machine Cookbook III
The Bread Machine Cookbook IV
The Bread Machine Cookbook V

Recipes for the Pressure Cooker
The New Blender Book
The Sandwich Maker Cookbook
Waffles
The Coffee Book
The Juicer Book
The Juicer Book II
Bread Baking (traditional), revised
The Kid's Cookbook
No Salt, No Sugar, No Fat Cookbook, revised
Cooking for 1 or 2, revised
Quick and Easy Pasta Recipes, revised
15-Minute Meals for 1 or 2
The 9x13 Pan Cookbook
Extra-Special Crockery Pot Recipes

Chocolate Cherry Tortes and Other Lowfat Delights
Low Fat American Favorites
Now That's Italian!
Fabulous Fiber Cookery
Low Salt, Low Sugar, Low Fat Desserts
Healthy Cooking on the Run, revised
Healthy Snacks for Kids
Muffins, Nut Breads and More
The Wok
New Ways to Enjoy Chicken
Favorite Seafood Recipes
New International Fondue Cookbook
Favorite Cookie Recipes
Authentic Mexican Cooking
Fisherman's Wharf Cookbook

Write or call for our free catalog.
BRISTOL PUBLISHING ENTERPRISES, INC.
P.O. Box 1737, San Leandro, CA 94577
(800) 346-4889; in California (510) 895-4461